SCHOLASTIC

Fractured Fairy Tales Fractions & Decimals

by Dan Greenberg

New York ❖ Toronto ❖ London ❖ Auckland ❖ Sydney
Mexico City ❖ New Delhi ❖ Hong Kong ❖ Buenos Aires

Teaching Resources

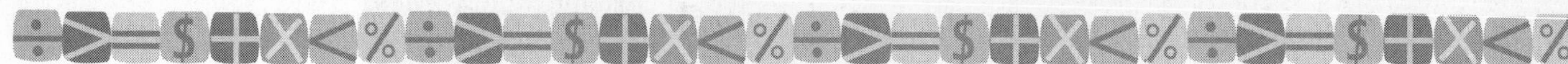

Cover design by Maria Lilja
Cover illustration by Doug Jones
Interior design by Kelli Thompson
Interior illustrations by Mike Moran

ISBN 0-439-51900-4

Printed in the U.S.A.

2 3 4 5 6 7 8 9 10 40 12 11 10 09 08

Contents

Contents

The 25 stories in *Fractured Fairy Tales: Fractions & Decimals* all have a single purpose: to teach fractions and decimals in an entertaining yet mathematically rigorous context. The stories themselves are based on familiar fairy tales, fables, and related concepts. However, they've all been transformed into something new and, we hope, very funny. For example, the Gingerbread Boy appears as a pro-football rookie, while Baa Baa Black Sheep is a hard-boiled crime reporter, and Little Red Riding Hood is a hip trumpet player looking for a recording contract.

Each story serves as a launching pad into a key mathematical concept. The book begins by introducing the concept of fractions, and uses visual examples to reinforce students' understanding of the material. From there, individual stories progress in skill level, moving through mixed numbers and improper fractions, to ordering fractions and decimals, to rounding decimals, and finally, to finding equivalent fractions, decimals, and percents—all the while using the basic operations: addition, subtraction, multiplication, and division. Each story provides model problems for students to work through before they begin their own computation.

Simple word problems as well as more complex problem-solving exercises are provided throughout the text. We've also included special topics such as subtracting mixed numbers with renaming, as well as solving multistep and proportion problems. Special emphasis in the book is placed on mental math and estimation, encouraging students to use these skills as checks for all kinds of calculations. You will find a complete answer key that starts on page 58.

We recommend the following ways to use these activities in the classroom:

- Whole class participation, in which students or the teacher read the story aloud, solve one or more model problem examples, and then solve problems individually.

- Small group participation, in which 2 to 5 individuals work together to master the material.

- Individual participation, in which students read the stories and solve the problems on their own.

We encourage students to engage the stories directly by writing their own responses, comments, and/or questions to events that take place in the text. One fun, cross-curricular option might have students write their own "fractured" fairy tales to complement the stories that they have read.

Overall, the stories in this book are intended to appeal to all kinds of learners—including students not easily motivated by traditional textbooks—making math learning fun and accessible for all.

NCTM Standards Grid

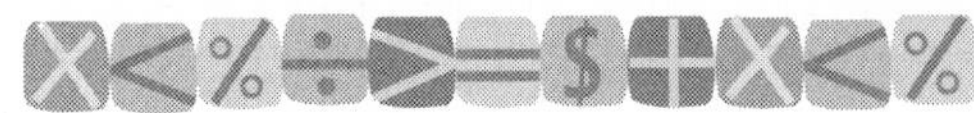

	Number and Operations	Algebra	Geometry	Measurement	Data Analysis and Probability	Problem Solving	Reasoning and Proof	Communication	Connections	Representation
Princess P Speaks Out	X	X			X	X	X	X	X	X
Interview With a Dragon	X	X				X	X	X	X	X
Cow Gets a Boat	X	X				X	X	X	X	X
Gingerbread Boy to Make Pro Debut	X	X		X		X	X	X	X	X
Why Cow Is Slow	X	X		X		X	X	X	X	X
Red Riding Hood	X	X		X		X	X	X	X	X
The Magic Parking Space	X	X		X		X	X	X	X	X
Sheep Gets a Scholarship	X	X				X	X	X	X	X
The Magic Racket	X	X		X		X	X	X	X	X
The Ugly Dumpling	X	X		X		X	X	X	X	X
King Doofus and the Bad Rock	X	X				X	X	X	X	X
Bed-Time Live: Cinderella	X	X				X	X	X	X	X
Judy Echo and Chuck Narcissus, Part 1	X	X		X		X	X	X	X	X
Judy Echo and Chuck Narcissus, Part 2	X	X		X		X	X	X	X	X
The Royal Ninny	X	X		X		X	X	X	X	X
Channel F Presents the Kissing Olympics	X			X		X	X	X	X	X
The Genie and the Three Wishes	X			X		X	X	X	X	X
The Baa Baa Report	X			X		X	X	X	X	X
The Quest for the Holly Gray-L	X					X	X	X	X	X
Wolf Guarding Henhouse to Resign	X	X			X	X	X	X	X	X
Great Hero and Total Coward	X	X			X	X	X	X	X	X
Why Owl Is Wise	X	X				X	X	X	X	X
Milton Bisk, Real Estate Agent to the Stars	X	X		X		X	X	X	X	X
Fairy Land Annual Poll	X					X	X	X	X	X
Wicked Witch of the South to Retire!	X	X				X	X	X	X	X

Name ______________________ Date __________

The Fairy Tale World's Greatest Newspaper

★ THE FRACTURED ★ FAIRY TALE GAZETTE

VOL. CLIII . . . . No. 55,554 Monday, September 24 $3.00

Princess P Speaks Out

A *Gazette* Exclusive
by Princess P

You've all seen the headline: PEA UPSETS SLEEP OF SPOILED PRINCESS. Well I'm the so-called spoiled princess. Let me say just one thing. *It's not what you think.*

That's right. Oh sure, I'll admit, I'm spoiled. Hey, I'm a *princess*! It's my *job* to be spoiled.

But here's how this thing with the pea all started. Mike's Mega-Mattress Superstore was looking to promote its new Soop-R-Pedic mattress.

So who better to get as a spokesperson than yours truly—a glamorous and very pampered princess. If someone as picky and coddled as I am can get a good night's sleep on this Soop-R-Pedic mattress, imagine how *normal* folks might feel!

Or something like that.

Model

Here are some peas for the princess. What fraction of the peas are dark? What fraction of the peas are light?

Three out of 5 peas are dark, or $\frac{3}{5}$.

Two out of 5 peas are light, or $\frac{2}{5}$.

1. Here is a second group of peas. What fraction of this group is dark?

____

2. What fraction is light?

____

So things are going fine. I'm snoozing away on the mattress. Mike's Mega-Mattress is filming the whole thing for their upcoming commercial. And then a strange thing happens: I start hearing these QUACKING noises.

And I'm like, *Hunh*?

Name ______________________ Date ____________

The Fractured Fairy Tale Gazette page 2

But when I look around, the whole castle is quiet. So I try to go back to sleep and the same thing happens again: QUACKING.

Hey, what's going on here?

In any event, I can't sleep. The next morning, everyone from Mike's is furious. It *couldn't* be the fault of their mattress, they insist. So they investigate, and sure enough, what do they find under the mattress? A single PEA. *That's* why I can't sleep!

The next morning, it's in all the headlines: SINGLE PEA SPOILS SLEEP OF SPOILED PRINCESS. All the nasty names they called me: SNOB. SNOOT. NINNY. You'd think I'd have committed a *crime*.

It didn't dawn on me that something was fishy until two days later. Castle security was doing a routine check when they found that the so-called *pea* was actually an electronic *transmitter*! And the quacking was being broadcast to keep me awake!

Who would do this? you ask. Try Nancy's Nighty-Night Bed Shop, Mike's arch rival. They wanted to make Mike's look bad—and they succeeded.

And so what's the upshot of all this? You're not going to believe it. Mike's mad and Nancy's Nighty-Night is in trouble. A third mattress store, Sweet Dream Sid's, has offered me a deal presenting the Super-Deluxe Princess Personal Pea Mattress.

Each Personal Pea Mattress comes with its own *pea*. That's right, under each mattress they're putting a single pea that the customer may or may not remove after the sale.

Is that a good gimmick or what?

THE END

3. What fraction of the ducks are dark?

____

4. What fraction of the ducks are light?

____

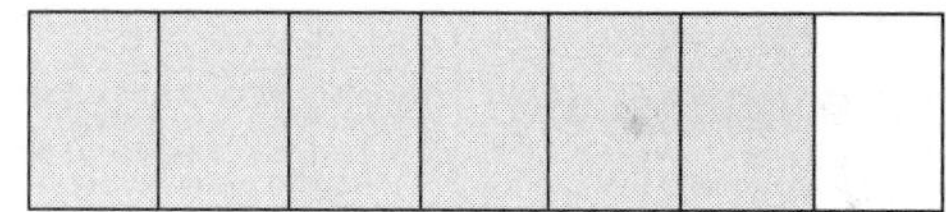

5. What fraction of the bar is colored in?

____

6. What fraction of the bar is not colored in?

____

7. Draw a group of peas to represent the fraction $\frac{3}{4}$.

8. Draw a group of peas to represent the fraction $\frac{3}{7}$.

Name ______________________ Date ______________

Interview With a Dragon

Hello, and welcome to The Big Interview on Channel F, the Fairy Tale Channel. I'm Pillow Jones, your host. Tonight on F, an interview with Chester, the Fire-Breathing Dragon.

Pillow: Good evening, Sir Dragon. Let's start at the beginning. How long have you been a dragon?

Dragon: Almost my entire career. I started out as a hideous monster. But then I quickly decided that being hideous was not what I wanted to do. I wanted to be a dragon.

Pillow: Any particular *kind* of dragon?

Dragon: Yes, the fire-breathing kind that frightened whole villages and destroyed large castles.

Pillow: And do you feel you've achieved that goal?

Dragon: More or less. Though I don't think people are quite as scared of dragons as they used to be.

Pillow: And why is that?

Dragon: I don't know. Video games? Overexposure? I'm not sure.

Pillow: Do others seem to feel this way as well?

Dragon: To a large degree. I've talked to my good friend Godzilla about it, and he seems to think it has something to do with cable TV. Again, I'm not sure.

Model

Four of every 6 dragons enjoys breathing fire.

Write the fraction $\frac{4}{6}$ in simplest form.

To simplify, divide both top and bottom by the same number.

$$\frac{4}{6} = \frac{4 \div 2}{6 \div 2} = \frac{2}{3}$$

Always try to divide by the largest number possible.

Write the fraction $\frac{2}{4}$ in simplest form.

$$\frac{2}{4} = \frac{2 \div ?}{4 \div ?} = \frac{?}{?}$$

Write each fraction in simplest form.

1. $\frac{3}{6}$ ______
2. $\frac{2}{6}$ ______
3. $\frac{3}{9}$ ______
4. $\frac{5}{10}$ ______
5. $\frac{4}{12}$ ______
6. $\frac{6}{8}$ ______

Simplifying Fractions

Name ______________________________ Date ______________

7. $\frac{8}{12}$ ______

8. $\frac{10}{15}$ ______

9. $\frac{9}{12}$ ______

10. $\frac{12}{15}$ ______

11. $\frac{8}{16}$ ______

12. $\frac{5}{20}$ ______

13. $\frac{12}{16}$ ______

14. $\frac{14}{21}$ ______

15. $\frac{8}{20}$ ______

16. $\frac{25}{30}$ ______

Pillow: What's your favorite thing to do as a dragon?

Dragon: Hmm, that's a toughie. I'm not sure where to start. I adore burning the straw rooftops off cottages with my fiery dragon breath. And I *love* the look on a knight in shining armor's face when he realizes how indestructible I am.

Pillow: Sounds like you enjoy being a dragon.

Dragon: I do. I love it, because it's fun. Each day is different. You have something new to destroy or someone new to scare.

Pillow: Any regrets about your career?

Dragon: Oh sure. Just once, I'd like to see the forces of evil come out on top. I mean, this whole thing is getting ridiculous. Just once, I'd like to see someone like me or Godzilla standing tall at the end of the day instead of lying in the dust.

Dragon: Is that your dream?

Pillow: I'd say so. Sure.

Dragon: Thank you very much, Chester. It's been interesting.

Pillow: Yes it has. Thank you. And to all my fans out there, thank you for your support!

THE END

To write a fraction in its simplest form, you may need to simplify more than once.

$$\frac{12}{60} = \frac{12 \div 6}{60 \div 6} = \frac{2}{10} \rightarrow \frac{2 \div 2}{10 \div 2} = \frac{1}{5}$$

Write each fraction in simplest form. Simplify more than once if necessary.

17. $\frac{16}{24}$ ______

18. $\frac{16}{40}$ ______

19. $\frac{32}{80}$ ______

20. $\frac{24}{56}$ ______

Name ______________________ Date ______________

Cow Gets a Boat

One day when Cow went down to the river she ran into Crocodile, who offered to sell her a boat.

"A boat?" Cow said. "What would a cow do with a boat?"

"Oh, you'll love life on the river," Croc said. "I can introduce you to some of my river pals. They're quite an amusing bunch."

"Hmm," thought Cow. Back in the field, she had never thought of her cow friends as very amusing. In fact, many of them seemed downright dull.

Now, buying a boat didn't seem like a bad idea.

"I'll take it," Cow said.

The next day, Cow packed a picnic basket containing lots of delicious hay sandwiches and went out to the river. At the boat launch, guess who Cow ran into?

"Crocodile!" Cow cried. "My old friend. How goes life on the river?"

Croc frowned. "Do I know you?" he asked.

"Of course!" said Cow. "I'm Cow. I bought this boat from you, remember? You were going to introduce me to some of your amusing river pals. I brought hay sandwiches for everyone."

"Oh right," said Croc. "Well, as you can see, I'm sort of busy right now."

But Croc and his pals didn't seem busy. They were just lolling around in the shallow water.

So Cow went off by herself in her new boat. After a while, she began to enjoy herself, when she suddenly heard some frantic splashing and shouting.

"Help!" cried a familiar voice.

"Who is it?" cried Cow.

Model

In her picnic basket, Cow brought two hay sandwiches weighing $\frac{2}{5}$ of a pound each. How much do two sandwiches weigh all together?

$$\frac{2}{5} + \frac{2}{5} = \frac{4}{5}$$

How much do sandwiches weighing $\frac{3}{5}$ of a pound and $\frac{4}{5}$ of a pound weigh in all?

$$\frac{3}{5} + \frac{4}{5} = \frac{7}{5} \rightarrow 7 \div 5 = 1\frac{2}{5} \text{ pounds}$$

Find each sum or difference.
Write each fraction in simplest form.

1. $\frac{2}{3} + \frac{2}{3} =$ ______

2. $\frac{4}{5} - \frac{1}{5} =$ ______

3. $\frac{3}{4} + \frac{1}{4} =$ ______

4. $\frac{6}{7} - \frac{4}{7} =$ ______

5. $\frac{5}{9} + \frac{8}{9} =$ ______

6. $\frac{5}{6} + \frac{1}{6} =$ ______

Name ______________________ Date __________

7. $\frac{8}{11} - \frac{6}{11} =$ ______

8. $\frac{11}{15} - \frac{2}{15} =$ ______

9. $\frac{4}{5} + \frac{2}{5} =$ ______

10. $\frac{10}{13} + \frac{5}{13} =$ ______

11. $\frac{15}{17} + \frac{9}{17} =$ ______

12. $\frac{8}{9} - \frac{4}{9} =$ ______

"It's me, Crocodile," said the voice. "I'm stuck in a net!"

"Do I know you?" asked Cow, with one eyebrow raised.

"Of course," Croc said. "I sold you your boat. And a fine boat it is. Aren't you enjoying it?"

"Very much," said Cow. "But weren't you going to introduce me to some of your amusing friends?"

"Oh, of course!" said Croc. "As soon as you get me out of this net. I'm sure they'll all like you."

At this point, Cow had to decide: should she help Croc out of the net or not?

Cow untangled the net. Croc swam free.

As Cow headed toward home, Croc cried, "Wait! Don't you want to meet some of my friends now? They're quite a lively bunch."

"No," Cow said. "I have my own friends."

That evening, back in the barn, Cow told the rest of the herd about her adventures on the river.

Suddenly, the other cows didn't seem so dull after all.

THE END

Model

How much do two sandwiches weighing $\frac{5}{8}$ pound and $\frac{7}{8}$ pound weigh altogether? In this, the sum must be simplified more than once.

$$\frac{5}{8} + \frac{7}{8} = \frac{12}{8} \rightarrow \frac{12}{8} = 1\frac{4}{8} \rightarrow 1\frac{4 \div 4}{8 \div 4} = 1\frac{1}{2}$$

Find each sum or difference. Write each fraction in simplest form. You may need to simplify after adding.

13. $\frac{3}{4} + \frac{3}{4} =$ ______

14. $\frac{7}{8} - \frac{3}{8} =$ ______

15. $\frac{5}{6} + \frac{5}{6} =$ ______

16. $\frac{5}{9} - \frac{2}{9} =$ ______

Name ______________________ Date ______________

Monday, September 24 **★ THE FRACTURED FAIRY TALE GAZETTE ★** page 1

Sports

Gingerbread Boy to Make Pro Debut— Will the Cookie Rookie Crumble?

by Itsy B. Spider

Around football training camp he's known simply as "G-Boy." And there's no doubt that this Gingerbread Boy can run. How fast is this rookie cookie? Baytown Brutes's coach Tom Roach said:

"The kid runs rings around our other wide receivers."

Indeed, Gingerbread Boy was clocked running the 40-yard dash in $\frac{2}{5}$ of a second. Compare that to the $4\frac{3}{5}$ second times turned in by normal wide receivers, and you'll see just how fast this rookie is.

But can a *cookie* play big-time professional football?

"That's the $64,000 question," Coach Roach said. "We've never had a cookie play on our team before."

Indeed, no cookies, cakes, pies, strudels, cinnamon buns, or pastry products of any type have played in the league since running back Cookie Gilchrist in the early 1960s, punter Jelly Roll Watson in the '50s, and tackle William "Bundt Cake" Berry in the '30s.

Model

One player ran the 40-yard dash in $4\frac{3}{5}$ seconds. What is $4\frac{3}{5}$ as an improper fraction?

Step 1: Multiply the whole number by the denominator.

Step 2: Add the numerator.

Step 3: Write the sum over the same denominator.

$$4\frac{3}{5} \rightarrow 4 \times 5 = 20 \rightarrow 20 + 3 = 23 \rightarrow \frac{23}{5}$$

(Step 1) (Step 2) (Step 3)

Write each mixed number as an improper fraction.

1. $1\frac{1}{4}$ ______
2. $2\frac{2}{3}$ ______
3. $3\frac{1}{5}$ ______
4. $4\frac{5}{6}$ ______
5. $3\frac{4}{7}$ ______
6. $5\frac{1}{8}$ ______
7. $9\frac{2}{3}$ ______
8. $12\frac{3}{8}$ ______

Mixed Numbers & Improper Fractions

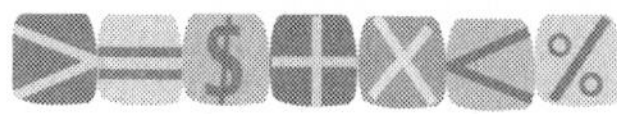

Name ______________________________ **Date** ______________

The Fractured Fairy Tale Gazette—SPORTS page 2

"You need to keep in mind," said G-Boy's agent, "Mom" Macy, "this kid is 100 percent gingerbread. But he ran away. He ran so fast I couldn't catch him. No one could catch him."

No one, that is, until Coach Roach of the Baytown Brutes offered Gingerbread Boy a $2 million no-cut contract.

That got his attention in a hurry.

Hopes are high for the speedy rookie, but questions remain. For one: Is Gingerbread Boy tough enough?

"This is one tough cookie," said Coach Roach. "If he were, for example, a chocolate chip cookie or a ginger snap I'd have my doubts. But this is a cookie who can definitely play with the big boys."

The coach's big worry? G-Boy's weight.

At only $\frac{8}{3}$ ounces, G-Boy weighs only a fraction of a pro wide receiver that weighs in at a solid 195 pounds.

"But he's well put-together for a cookie," said Mom Macy. "I know because I made him myself."

This reporter's opinion? This Cookie Rookie may well put it all together. But what happens when a 250-pound linebacker lays into that soft gingerbread dough?

Will he cave?

Will his act get stale?

Will the cookie rookie crumble?

Stay tuned, folks. It's going to be an interesting season.

THE END

Model

What is the Gingerbread Boy's weight, $\frac{8}{3}$ ounces, as a mixed number?

Step 1: Divide the numerator by the denominator.

Step 2: Write the remainder as a fraction.

$$\begin{array}{r} 2\tfrac{2}{3} \\ 3\overline{)8} \\ -6 \\ \hline 2 \end{array}$$

Write each improper fraction as a mixed number.

9. $\frac{3}{2}$ ________

10. $\frac{5}{4}$ ________

11. $\frac{7}{3}$ ________

12. $\frac{9}{4}$ ________

13. $\frac{10}{3}$ ________

14. $\frac{20}{7}$ ________

15. $\frac{25}{4}$ ________

16. $\frac{15}{13}$ ________

17. $\frac{50}{11}$ ________

18. $\frac{100}{23}$ ________

Name ______________________________ Date ______________

Why Cow Is Slow

A long time ago, Cow was a lot more *speedy* than she is today. Actually, Cow was quite sleek and beautiful. In fact, Cow was so sleek and beautiful that everyone was always chasing after her.

After a time, Cow began to wish she could be a little less sleek and be left alone. But to no avail, until she met the Good Cow Fairy.

"Oh, Good Cow Fairy," Cow said. "I am tired of being the way I am. I wish I could be something else."

"Your wish is my command," said the Good Cow Fairy, who was also known as the GCF.

Sure enough, the GCF turned Cow into a princess, a sleek and beautiful young princess. And soon she was being chased by a host of dull young princes.

There was Prince Drudge, who droned on and on—always talking about himself, never asking a single question about her.

"Do you find me dull?" the Prince asked.

"Yes!" replied Princess Cow.

There was Prince Boast, who spoke only of his own achievements, which were not very great or interesting.

"Do you find me stuck up?" asked Boast.

"Extremely!" replied Princess Cow.

There was Prince Cash, who endlessly talked of budgets, pie charts, statistics, and other money matters.

"Are you listening to me?" he asked, after another long economic session.

"No!" cried the princess, enthusiastically.

Model

Prince Drudge talked for $\frac{1}{4}$ of an hour about his sock collection. Then he talked for $\frac{1}{6}$ of an hour about his new haircut. How long did he talk in all?

$$\frac{1}{4} + \frac{1}{6} =$$

Step 1: Find the least common multiple (LCM) of the two denominators, 4 and 6.

4: 4, 8, (12), 16   6: 6, (12), 18   LCM = 12

Step 2: Use the LCM as your lowest common denominator (LCD).

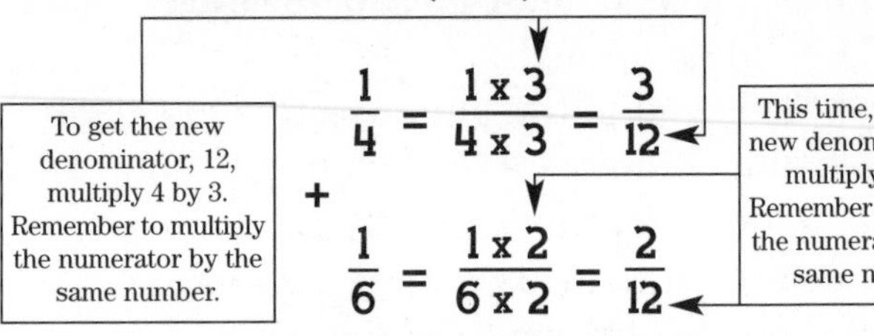

Step 3: Add the products.

$$\frac{3}{12} + \frac{2}{12} = \frac{5}{12}$$

Answer: He talked for $\frac{5}{12}$ of an hour.

Find the LCM for each fraction pair.

1. $\frac{1}{2}, \frac{2}{3}$ ______

2. $\frac{1}{4}, \frac{1}{2}$ ______

3. $\frac{1}{3}, \frac{3}{5}$ ______

4. $\frac{3}{8}, \frac{3}{4}$ ______

Adding & Subtracting With Unlike Denominators

Name ______________________ Date ____________

Use the LCM to find each sum or difference. Make sure that your answers are in simplest form.

5. $\frac{1}{2} + \frac{1}{3} =$ _______

6. $\frac{1}{4} + \frac{2}{3} =$ _______

7. $\frac{5}{6} + \frac{1}{8} =$ _______

8. $\frac{5}{8} + \frac{1}{4} =$ _______

9. $\frac{5}{9} - \frac{1}{6} =$ _______

10. $\frac{5}{6} - \frac{5}{7} =$ _______

It got to the point where Princess Cow was ready to scream.

"Can't they leave me alone?" she asked. "Why must I be such a sleek and beautiful princess?"

Apparently, the Good Cow Fairy heard all this and granted Cow's wish.

"I hereby turn you back into a cow," the GCF said. "Only this time you will be neither sleek, nor beautiful. In fact, you will be as stout as a barrel. You will stand in one place and chew your cud, swatting flies with a blank look in your eyes."

"Anything to get away from those dull princes," said Cow.

And so it happened. Cow became a slow, plodding creature. No longer sleek or beautiful, she was content to roam the fields, chew her cud, and swat flies. No one chased her, or bored her, or pestered her.

And today, Cow still has the same slow, deliberate manner. There is no doubt that is the result of being bothered for all those years. She is no longer in a hurry to get away.

THE END

11. Prince Boast bragged that he ran $\frac{3}{5}$ of a mile on Tuesday. Then he ran $\frac{1}{4}$ of a mile on Wednesday. How far did the prince run in all?

____

12. Prince Boast also bragged about the fish that he caught. On Thursday he caught a blue fish that was $\frac{3}{4}$ foot long. On Friday he caught a trout that was $\frac{1}{2}$ foot long. How much longer was the blue fish?

____

13. Prince Cash spends $\frac{5}{8}$ of his day counting his money and $\frac{1}{10}$ of the day spending his money. What fraction of the day does he use to count and spend?

____

14. Cow spent $\frac{4}{7}$ of the morning grazing and $\frac{2}{5}$ of the morning chewing her cud. How much longer did she spend grazing?

____

Name ______________________________ Date ______________

Red Riding Hood

Once upon a time there was a *fabulous* trumpet player named Red Riding Hood. Red had an okay recording contract with O.K. Records. But another company named Lone Wolf, Inc. was trying to get Red to sign with them.

One day Red's manager Doggie Jones got a call from a hot night club named Grannie's.

"Dig it," Doggie said. (Doggie spoke a strange language called Hip Talk.) "You've got a fat gig at Grannie's."

(Translation: *Red had a musical job.*)

"You better split, like yesterday," Doggie said.

(Translation: *Go there right away.*)

So Red hailed a cab. The driver looked familiar to her.

"Greetings," he said. "Where you headed?"

"To Grannie's," Red said. "I've got a musical gig there. I play trumpet."

"You're pulling my leg," the driver said.

"No I'm not," Red said, but she did notice that he had four of them—legs, that is—which was unusual for a cab driver.

Model

Red was scheduled to play two sets at Grannie's lasting $3\frac{3}{4}$ hours and $2\frac{5}{6}$ hours. How long would she play in all?

Step 1: Add whole numbers and fractions separately. Use the LCD.

$$3\frac{3}{4} = \frac{3 \times 3}{4 \times 3} = \frac{9}{12}$$

$$+\ 2\frac{5}{6} = \frac{5 \times 2}{6 \times 2} = \frac{10}{12}$$

$$5 \qquad \frac{19}{12}$$

Step 2: Change $\frac{19}{12}$ from an improper fraction to a fraction. Add.

$$5 + \frac{19}{12} = 5 + 1\frac{7}{12} = 6\frac{7}{12}$$

Calculate and write each fraction in simplest form.

1. $2\frac{1}{3} + 3\frac{2}{5}$

2. $4\frac{3}{8} + 1\frac{5}{8}$

3. $6\frac{4}{5} + 2\frac{1}{4}$

4. $5\frac{5}{8} + 4\frac{3}{4}$

Name ______________________________ **Date** ______________

5. $\begin{array}{r} 7\frac{4}{5} \\ -\ 6\frac{5}{9} \\ \hline \end{array}$

6. $\begin{array}{r} 3\frac{3}{10} \\ +\ 4\frac{4}{5} \\ \hline \end{array}$

7. $\begin{array}{r} 6\frac{5}{12} \\ +\ 9\frac{5}{8} \\ \hline \end{array}$

8. $\begin{array}{r} 10\frac{4}{5} \\ -\ 7\frac{7}{15} \\ \hline \end{array}$

The driver dropped Red off at Grannie's. It took awhile for Grannie to come out. Grannie wore cool shades over his eyes and a pork-pie hat that covered half his face.

"Hello, Grannie," Red said. "I'm Red Riding Hood, the trumpet player. Do you speak English or Hip Talk?"

"Both," Grannie said. "Come closer so I can dig your vibes."

Red came closer. In fact, she came so close that she could actually *see* the recording contracts on Grannie's desk.

"Oh Grannie, what a lot of contracts you've got," Red said.

"The better to sign up new talent with," Grannie said.

Red looked at the dollar amounts on the contracts.

"Oh Grannie," Red said, "what *big* contracts you've got."

"The better to lure talent away from two-bit companies like O.K. Records with," Grannie said.

Red looked at the name on the top of the contracts: *Lone Wolf.*

"Oh Grannie," Red said, "what a well-known recording company you represent."

"The better to *gobble you up*!" Grannie said, lunging forward so his sunglasses and hat fell off.

"Hey, you're not Grannie!" Red cried. "You're the cab driver."

Without missing a beat, the driver handed Red his card, which revealed that he was really George Wolf, President of Lone Wolf Records, Inc.

And with that, the two proceeded to call their lawyers. In a short time, they were able to hammer out a recording contract that made Red Riding Hood a very *wealthy* and *happy* young musician.

The moral of the story? Sometimes it's not so bad to get gobbled up!

THE END

9. On her CD, Red's recording of her new song, "What Big Eyes You've Got," lasted $6\frac{3}{8}$ minutes. The live version of the song lasted $7\frac{2}{3}$ minutes. How much longer was the live version?

____

10. Each night, Grannie's featured a comedy performance that lasted $1\frac{5}{8}$ hours and a singer who sang for $1\frac{3}{5}$ hours. How long did these two performances last in all?

____

11. Red's $31\frac{3}{8}$ inch trumpet was $2\frac{1}{2}$ inches shorter than the trumpet played by Slim Charlie Perkins. How long was Slim Charlie's trumpet?

____

12. Slim Charlie put a $36\frac{7}{8}$ inch belt around his $23\frac{1}{12}$ inch waist. How much bigger was the belt than Slim's waist?

____

Fractured Fairy Tales: Fractions & Decimals • Scholastic Teaching Resources

Name ______________________ Date ______________

The Magic Parking Space

Wanda was a waitress at Cha-Cha's Grille. She worked hard for her money. So when Wanda had finally saved up enough to buy a car, she was proud of herself.

She was also very happy with the car, until it was time to park the thing. Cha-Cha's was located right downtown, so there was *never* anyplace to park. It seemed like Wanda would drive around *forever*, searching for a spot. In fact, one evening, it took so long that Wanda arrived late at the restaurant. She rushed over to Table 3 where her favorite customer, Mr. Ponds, was waiting.

"I'm sorry I'm late," Wanda said. "It won't happen again."

"You can say that again, Wanda," Mr. Ponds said. "You won't *ever* need to worry about a parking space again."

Wanda smiled. Mr. Ponds, a sweet gentleman, was kind, considerate, and an excellent tipper! But how could he *guarantee* a parking space? Nobody could do that.

Nonetheless, the next day the only parking space available on the street was much too small, but somehow Wanda fit right into it! Like magic!

When Wanda got to Cha-Cha's, Mr. Ponds was waiting. "You'll never guess what happened," Wanda said.

"You found a parking space," Mr. Ponds said.

"Why yes," said Wanda. "How did you know?"

Mr. Ponds smiled.

Model

A parking space measures 14 feet in length. How much extra space will a $12\frac{2}{3}$ foot long car have in this space?

Step 1: Think of 14 as 13 + 1.

$$\begin{array}{rcr} 14 & = & 13 + 1 \\ -12\frac{2}{3} & = & -12\frac{2}{3} \\ \hline \end{array}$$

Step 2: Change the 1 to $\frac{3}{3}$. Subtract.

$$\begin{array}{r} 13\frac{3}{3} \\ -12\frac{2}{3} \\ \hline 1\frac{1}{3} \text{ feet} \end{array}$$

Calculate and write each fraction in simplest form.

1. $\begin{array}{r} 5 \\ -3\frac{1}{2} \\ \hline \end{array}$

2. $\begin{array}{r} 4 \\ -1\frac{5}{8} \\ \hline \end{array}$

3. $\begin{array}{r} 6 \\ -2\frac{1}{4} \\ \hline \end{array}$

4. $\begin{array}{r} 5 \\ -1\frac{3}{4} \\ \hline \end{array}$

Subtracting Mixed Numbers With Renaming

Name ______________________________ **Date** ______________

5. $\begin{array}{r} 10 \\ -7\frac{5}{9} \\ \hline \end{array}$

6. $\begin{array}{r} 13 \\ -4\frac{4}{5} \\ \hline \end{array}$

7. $\begin{array}{r} 16 \\ -9\frac{5}{8} \\ \hline \end{array}$

8. $\begin{array}{r} 10 \\ -7\frac{7}{15} \\ \hline \end{array}$

The same thing happened for the next five days. Each day, Wanda somehow was able to fit into a parking space that no other car could fit into.

This was getting spooky.

Finally, Wanda came to Mr. Ponds and *demanded* to know what was going on.

"I'm your Fairy Parking Godfather," Mr. Ponds said.

"Fairy *Parking* Godfather?" Wanda said.

Mr. Ponds explained. A Fairy Parking Godfather was just like any other Fairy Godfather. But his powers were limited to parking spaces.

"It's just my luck," Wanda said. "Of all the magical spells in the world that might make a person rich or powerful or famous—this is what I get: a *magic parking space*."

Mr. Ponds laughed, "What can I say? As a Fairy Parking Godfather, I may not make you rich or powerful—but I *do* give something that even the rich and powerful don't always have—a place to put your car. And when you think about it—that's not bad."

So Wanda did think about it, and she decided that Mr. Ponds was right. A good parking space wasn't bad. It wasn't bad at all.

THE END

Model

Wanda worked $8\frac{1}{3}$ hours on Wednesday. She worked $5\frac{5}{6}$ hours on Thursday. How much longer did she work on Wednesday?

Step 1: Find the LCD.

$$\begin{array}{rcr} 8\frac{1}{3} & = & 8\frac{2}{6} \\ -5\frac{5}{6} & = & -5\frac{5}{6} \\ \hline \end{array}$$

Step 2: Think of 8 as 7 + 1 or $7\frac{6}{6}$. Combine with $\frac{2}{6}$.

$$8\frac{2}{6} = 7 + \frac{6}{6} + \frac{2}{6} = 7\frac{8}{6}$$

$$\begin{array}{r} -5\frac{5}{6} \\ \hline \end{array}$$

Step 3: Subtract and simplify.

$$\begin{array}{r} 7\frac{8}{6} \\ -5\frac{5}{6} \\ \hline 2\frac{3}{6} \end{array} = 2\frac{1}{2} \text{ hours}$$

Find each difference. Simplify.

9. $\begin{array}{r} 6\frac{1}{3} \\ -4\frac{2}{3} \\ \hline \end{array}$

10. $\begin{array}{r} 3\frac{1}{4} \\ -1\frac{3}{4} \\ \hline \end{array}$

11. $\begin{array}{r} 5\frac{2}{5} \\ -3\frac{7}{10} \\ \hline \end{array}$

12. $\begin{array}{r} 9\frac{3}{14} \\ -1\frac{5}{7} \\ \hline \end{array}$

Name ______________________ Date ______________

Sheep Gets a Scholarship

Once there was a Sheep who was a very good student in Sheep School. She did well in all of her school subjects, including Reading, Writing, Math, and Grazing.

So when it came time for college, Sheep got all sorts of excellent offers. Sheep State College and Goat Tech both offered small scholarships. Wolf University, on the other hand, offered a full scholarship—all expenses paid.

"Wolf University?" Sheep thought. "Why would they want me?" Wolf was one of the finest—and most expensive—schools in the country.

"Because you're a sheep," Wolf's Dean of Admissions told her, when she called to find out.

"But what would I do in a school for wolves?" Sheep asked.

"We have a fine swimming pool," the Dean told her.

"Sheep don't swim," Sheep said.

"Our Hunting program is top-rated," said the Dean.

"Sheep don't hunt," Sheep said.

"Why don't you come and visit the campus?" the Dean said. "Then you can see for yourself."

So Sheep came to visit. How well she was treated! All of the campus big-wigs came to see her.

"You'll fit in great here," they all told her.

"Where are all the other sheep?" asked Sheep.

"Oh, they're probably in their rooms studying," the Dean said.

At the end of her visit, the Dean took Sheep to a beautiful pasture in the center of the campus.

"If you come to Wolf U," the Dean said, "this entire pasture will be yours. All yours."

This was impressive. At Sheep State and Goat Tech, Sheep would need to share a pasture with many others.

Model

At Sheep State, $\frac{2}{5}$ of a 20-acre field were reserved for the freshman sheep. How many acres did the freshman get in all?

Step 1: Write the problem.

$$20 \times \frac{2}{5} =$$

Step 2: Write whole numbers over 1.

$$\frac{20}{1} \times \frac{2}{5} =$$

Step 3: Simplify, if possible.

$$\frac{\overset{4}{\cancel{20}}}{1} \times \frac{2}{\underset{1}{\cancel{5}}} =$$

Step 4: Multiply. Simplify again, if necessary.

$$\frac{\overset{4}{\cancel{20}}}{1} \times \frac{2}{\underset{1}{\cancel{5}}} = \frac{8}{1} = 8 \text{ acres}$$

Find each product.

1. $10 \times \frac{1}{2} =$ ______

2. $15 \times \frac{1}{3} =$ ______

3. $21 \times \frac{2}{3} =$ ______

4. $18 \times \frac{1}{6} =$ ______

Name ______________________ Date ____________

5. $15 \times \frac{3}{5} =$ ______

6. $\frac{3}{4} \times 24 =$ ______

7. $36 \times \frac{5}{6} =$ ______

8. $\frac{3}{8} \times 32 =$ ______

Model

At Wolf U, $\frac{5}{9}$ of the pasture was given to the sheep. The sheep used $\frac{6}{7}$ of this area for grazing. What fraction of the pasture did they use for grazing?

Step 1: Write the problem. Look for the common factors of the numerator of one fraction and the denominator of the other fraction.

$$\frac{5}{9} \times \frac{6}{7} =$$

Step 2: Find the greatest common factor.

GCF: 6: 2, (3), 6 9: (3), 9 (GCF = 3)

Step 3: Now simplify, using the GCF.

$$\frac{5}{9} \times \frac{6}{7} =$$

6 ÷ 3 → 2; 9 ÷ 3 → 3

Step 4: Multiply the numbers that are left.

$$\frac{5}{3} \times \frac{2}{7} = \frac{10}{21}$$

Find each product. Make sure that your answers are in simplest form.

9. $\frac{2}{5} \times \frac{5}{7} =$ ______

10. $\frac{5}{6} \times \frac{4}{9} =$ ______

11. $\frac{1}{3} \times \frac{2}{7} =$ ______

12. $\frac{5}{12} \times \frac{8}{15} =$ ______

13. $\frac{14}{15} \times \frac{10}{21} =$ ______

14. $\frac{10}{27} \times \frac{9}{25} =$ ______

15. $\frac{16}{21} \times \frac{7}{24} =$ ______

16. $\frac{24}{25} \times \frac{5}{32} =$ ______

17. $\frac{14}{15} \times \frac{25}{42} =$ ______

18. $\frac{27}{28} \times \frac{7}{45} =$ ______

As Sheep began to graze on the rich grass, she suddenly heard a sound.

"What was that?" she said. "It sounded like a howl."

"Oh, don't be ridiculous," said the Dean. "It was probably just some sophomores playing a prank."

"I think I'd better go now," said Sheep.

Sheep made her decision that night when she got home. Sheep State perhaps did not have the best library or the best swimming pool or her own private pasture. But somehow, Sheep felt that she would fit in better there.

And she was right.

THE END

Name ______________________________ Date ______________

The Magic Racket

Gigi had always been something of a daydreamer. So when she and her friend Pumpkin went to see tennis champ Martina Jones play a match, guess what happened? After the match, the champ tossed her souvenir racket into the crowd. Guess who caught it? Gigi!

"Oooh, bee-yoo-tiful!" cooed Pumpkin. "What a racket!"

Gigi was convinced that the racket was magic. And that if she played with this racket, no one would beat her.

No one!

There was only one problem.

"You don't even know how to *play* tennis," Pumpkin reminded her friend.

Model

Suppose Gigi practices tennis $2\frac{2}{3}$ hours a day for 6 days a week. In all, how many practice hours is this?

Step 1: Write the problem.

$$2\frac{2}{3} \times 6 =$$

Step 2: Change mixed numbers to improper fractions.

$$\frac{8}{3} \times \frac{6}{1} =$$

Step 3: Simplify, then multiply.

$$\frac{8}{\cancel{3}_1} \times \frac{\cancel{6}^2}{1} = \frac{8}{1} \times \frac{2}{1} = 16 \text{ hours}$$

Find each product. Make sure that your answers are in simplest form.

1. $1\frac{1}{4} \times 4 =$ ______
2. $2\frac{1}{3} \times 6 =$ ______
3. $8 \times 4\frac{1}{2} =$ ______
4. $10 \times 1\frac{2}{5} =$ ______
5. $1\frac{1}{6} \times 3 =$ ______
6. $1\frac{3}{8} \times 12 =$ ______
7. $4\frac{4}{5} \times \frac{5}{6} =$ ______
8. $2\frac{7}{9} \times \frac{3}{5} =$ ______

That was "no big thing," Gigi insisted. After all, she could learn. She could picture it all right now: *a bright day, a cheering stadium, a stunning victory in the World Championships using her magic racket.*

Game! *Set*! *Match*!

From there she'd have endorsements, movie contracts, the whole enchilada. Of course, she would no doubt marry some handsome tennis pro along the way, and they would have a child.

And of course, the time would come when the champion would pass along the magic racket to her young daughter.

"*I want to show you something, darling,*" she heard herself say to her imaginary daughter. "*I got this racket from a great champion many years ago.*"

Multiplying With Mixed Numbers

Name ______________________________ **Date** ____________

And of course, as children often do, the little one would make a grab for the famous racket.

"*No, no, no, darling*!" Gigi would say to the beautiful imaginary child, pulling the racket away rather briskly.

And of course, the actual racket Gigi was holding in her hand all this time while she was daydreaming was NOT imaginary at all—it was real.

And as she jerked it away from her imagined child, this very real (but perhaps not so magical) racket knocked into the fence, fell out of Gigi's hand, and bounced down the steps, making a series of horrid clunks that sent a burst of broken strings in all directions.

"Oh my goodness!" cried Pumpkin. "You broke your magic racket! Too bad!"

Too bad indeed. Though Gigi didn't say it, quite a bit more than a mere racket had just been broken.

THE END

Model

Gigi drank 2 $\frac{1}{4}$ bottles of Vita-Pro Health Water during her first tennis match. Each bottle contains 9 $\frac{1}{3}$ ounces. How many ounces did Gigi drink?

Step 1: Write the problem.

$$2\frac{1}{4} \text{ x } 9\frac{1}{3} =$$

Step 2: Change mixed numbers to improper fractions.

$$\frac{9}{4} \text{ x } \frac{28}{3} =$$

Step 3: Simplify, then multiply.

$$\frac{\overset{3}{\cancel{9}}}{\underset{1}{4}} \text{ x } \frac{\overset{7}{\cancel{28}}}{\underset{1}{\cancel{3}}} = 21 \text{ ounces}$$

Find each product. Make sure that your answers are in simplest form.

9. $3\frac{1}{3} \text{ x } 4\frac{1}{2} =$ ______

10. $3\frac{1}{5} \text{ x } 3\frac{1}{8} =$ ______

11. $1\frac{5}{7} \text{ x } 1\frac{3}{4} =$ ______

12. $1\frac{1}{9} \text{ x } 1\frac{1}{5} =$ ______

13. $3\frac{3}{5} \text{ x } 3\frac{8}{9} =$ ______

14. $2\frac{2}{9} \text{ x } 3\frac{3}{5} =$ ______

15. $1\frac{5}{16} \text{ x } 2\frac{2}{7} =$ ______

16. $9\frac{1}{3} \text{ x } 2\frac{1}{10} =$ ______

17. After practice, Gigi ate $2\frac{2}{5}$ bags of Health-Nut Trail Mix. Each bag contained $1\frac{1}{6}$ ounces of Trail Mix. How many ounces of Trail Mix did Gigi eat?

____

Dividing With Mixed Numbers

Name ______________________ Date ____________

The Ugly Dumpling

It was soup time in the kitchen. One by one the dumplings plopped into the steaming broth. Here was a nice one, another nice one, a third, a fourth—except—what was this? *One of the dumplings was incredibly ugly*!

An *ugly dumpling*. How ugly was this dumpling?

"It doesn't look like any dumpling I know," said one of the big dumplings.

"It looks like a monster from outer space," joked another.

"What do you know about monsters from outer space?" said a third. "After all, you're only a dumpling!"

Indeed, dumplings were not known for their brains. Little more than flour, egg, and milk, dumplings were simple beings, but they did know *ugly* when they saw it.

And this dumpling was ugly!

So they laughed. They laughed and laughed at this odd newcomer.

Only one dumpling took pity on the Ugly Dumpling. This kindly dumpling's name was Jerry.

"You're not so bad," said Jerry. "I've never seen a dumpling float so well. Where'd you learn to float like that?"

The Ugly Dumpling was quiet. Slowly, it started to drift toward the other end of the pot.

"I don't blame you," Jerry said. "If the other dumplings laughed at me, I'd leave too."

Jerry paused. "You know," he said, "I read a story once about an Ugly Duckling. It grew up to be a beautiful swan."

The Ugly Dumpling didn't say anything.

"And I know you'll grow up to be beautiful too," Jerry said. "For a dumpling."

Suddenly, the dumplings heard a voice: "Soup's on everyone!"

Model

To make dumplings, the cook divided a $3\frac{3}{4}$ ounce package of flour into 5 equal scoops. How big was each scoop?

Step 1: Write the problem.

$$3\frac{3}{4} \div 5 =$$

Step 2: Change mixed numbers to improper fractions. Invert the divisor.

$$\frac{15}{4} \div \frac{5}{1} \rightarrow \frac{15}{4} \times \frac{1}{5}$$

Step 3: Simplify, then multiply.

$$\frac{\overset{3}{\cancel{15}}}{4} \times \frac{1}{\underset{1}{\cancel{5}}} = \frac{3}{4} \times \frac{1}{1} = \frac{3}{4} \text{ ounces}$$

Find each quotient. Make sure that your answers are in simplest form.

1. $\frac{2}{3} \div 2 =$ ______
2. $1\frac{3}{4} \div 7 =$ ______
3. $12\frac{1}{2} \div 5 =$ ______
4. $3\frac{3}{5} \div 6 =$ ______
5. $2\frac{1}{7} \div 5 =$ ______
6. $2\frac{2}{9} \div 4 =$ ______
7. $4\frac{4}{5} \div 3 =$ ______
8. $7\frac{1}{7} \div 20 =$ ______

Fractured Fairy Tales: Fractions & Decimals • Scholastic Teaching Resources

Dividing With Mixed Numbers

Name ______________________________ Date ______________

It was the cook. All of the dumplings assembled, ready to be ladled.

Then the cook cried, "There it is! I've been looking all over for this kitchen sponge! It fell into the soup."

The cook fished the "Ugly Dumpling" out of the pot and placed it on the counter.

"You're not an Ugly Dumpling!" Jerry exclaimed. "You're a sponge—a kitchen sponge!"

And so, the Ugly Dumpling was returned to the countertop. And from then on, it lived a happy life, cleaning, wiping, and scrubbing, just like all of the other sponges.

But every once in a while, thoughts came to mind of the time spent as a dumpling—and of Jerry—and of the steaming hot broth!

Every once in a while, but not too often.

THE END

Model

The cook used a ladle that held $3\frac{1}{3}$ ounces to ladle out a pot that contained $11\frac{2}{3}$ ounces of soup. How many times would the cook need to ladle to empty the pot?

Step 1: Write the problem.

$$11\frac{2}{3} \div 3\frac{1}{3} =$$

Step 2: Change mixed numbers to improper fractions. Invert the divisor.

$$\frac{35}{3} \div \frac{10}{3} \rightarrow \frac{35}{3} \times \frac{3}{10}$$

Step 3: Simplify, then multiply.

$$\frac{\overset{7}{\cancel{35}}}{\underset{1}{\cancel{3}}} \times \frac{\overset{1}{\cancel{3}}}{\underset{2}{\cancel{10}}} = \frac{7}{1} \times \frac{1}{2} = \frac{7}{2} = 3\frac{1}{2}$$

Find each quotient. Make sure that your answers are in simplest form.

9. $6 \div 1\frac{2}{3} =$ ______

10. $2\frac{1}{4} \div 1\frac{1}{2} =$ ______

11. $2\frac{2}{5} \div 1\frac{1}{5} =$ ______

12. $2\frac{1}{10} \div 1\frac{2}{5} =$ ______

13. $4\frac{4}{5} \div 2\frac{2}{15} =$ ______

14. $1\frac{11}{49} \div 2\frac{1}{7} =$ ______

15. $1\frac{17}{64} \div 1\frac{13}{32} =$ ______

16. $1\frac{37}{63} \div 1\frac{4}{21}$ ______

17. The cook mixed $22\frac{1}{2}$ ounces of dumpling dough. How many dumplings can he make that weigh $1\frac{1}{4}$ ounces each?

____

18. How many $4\frac{4}{9}$ ounce bowls of soup can the cook pour from a pot that contains $26\frac{2}{3}$ ounces of soup?

____

Name ______________________________ Date ______________

King Doofus and the Bad Rock

Good King Doofus was not too bright. While hunting in the forest he saw a deer. He tried to catch it, but it ran far ahead.

"Hark!" cried King Doofus. "Why am I so slow and the deer so fast?"

The king sat and thought about this for awhile. Then he came up with a reason: shoes and socks. Deer did not wear them. People did. So deer were fast and people were slow.

"I shall taketh off my shoes and socks, and thereby become as speedy as the deer," said the king.

So the king took off his shoes and socks and once again dashed after the deer. Now, the deer got even farther ahead.

Plus, running barefoot, the king stubbed his toe on a rock!

"Zounds!" cried the King. "That smarteth, big time!"

When he returned to the castle, the king did three things. First, he issued a royal decree: *All animals in the kingdom must now weareth shoes and socks at all times.*

Next, the king arrested the rock he'd stubbed his toe on. Finally, he had the rock locked up in the royal prison.

"That'll teacheth you, bad rock!" he said to the rock.

Model

The king stubbed his toe on a rock that weighed 3.7 kilograms. What is this weight as a fraction? To find the fraction equivalent to decimals, look at the place value chart.

$$3.7 = 3\frac{7}{10}$$

___	___	3 .	7	___	___
hundredths place **100**	tens place **10**	ones place **1**	tenths place **0.1**	hundredths place **0.01**	thousandths place **0.001**

The decimal 3.7 has a 3 in the ones place and a 7 in the tenths place. So it is equal to $3\frac{7}{10}$.

Here are some other examples:

$0.7 = \frac{7}{10}$	$4.5 = 4\frac{5}{10}$	$603.8 = 603\frac{8}{10}$
$0.07 = \frac{7}{100}$	$4.05 = 4\frac{5}{100}$	$60.38 = 60\frac{38}{100}$
$0.007 = \frac{7}{1000}$	$4.005 = 4\frac{5}{1000}$	$60.038 = 60\frac{38}{1000}$

Write each decimal number in fraction form.

1. 0.6 _______
2. 1.4 _______
3. 0.2 _______
4. 8.3 _______
5. 0.14 _______
6. 2.65 _______
7. 0.37 _______
8. 28.59 _______
9. 0.03 _______
10. 2.004 _______
11. 583.046 _______
12. 0.076 _______

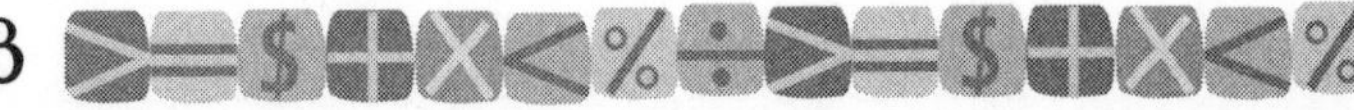

Name ______________________________ Date ______________

Each day the king returned to the prison cell and asked the rock:

"Well, Master Rock, have you learned your lesson?"

The rock, of course, said nothing.

One day the king announced:

"I've had a change of heart, Master Rock. You may have stubbed my toe, but I've come to admire your quiet and steadfast ways. Starting now, I hereby freeth you and appoint you as the new Prime Minister."

The bad rock said nothing.

So the king had it thrown back in prison.

The pattern continued. In and out of prison the bad rock went, never changing its silent, stubborn ways.

Finally, King Doofus grew tired of the whole affair, brought the bad rock back to the forest, tossed it on the ground, and said:

"I wisheth I had never bumped into you in the first place."

The bad rock said nothing. (After all, it was only a rock!)

At this point, the king once again saw a deer running through the forest and gave chase. The deer started to get away, but this time something was different—something was slowing down the deer. Over its hooves, the deer was wearing a small, but well-made pair of shoes and socks.

"Now I've gotteth you!" cried the king.

THE END

Model

Another rock $2\frac{3}{100}$ Kg. What is this number as a decimal?

Use the place value chart to turn fractions into decimals. Write a 2 in the ones place and a 3 in the hundredths place. Since there are no tenths, write a 0 in the tenths place.

$$2\frac{3}{100} = 2.03$$

____	____	____ .	____	____	____
hundredths place **100**	tens place **10**	ones place **1**	tenths place **0.1**	hundredths place **0.01**	thousandths place **0.001**

Write each fraction number in decimal form.

13. $\frac{5}{10}$ ______

14. $4\frac{4}{10}$ ______

15. $\frac{24}{100}$ ______

16. $6\frac{3}{10}$ ______

17. $\frac{4}{100}$ ______

18. $13\frac{45}{100}$ ______

19. $9\frac{6}{1000}$ ______

20. $241\frac{3}{100}$ ______

21. $\frac{18}{1000}$ ______

22. $2\frac{41}{100}$ ______

23. $376\frac{37}{1000}$ ______

24. $82\frac{1}{1000}$ ______

Name ______________________________ Date ______________

Bed-Time Live: Cinderella

Did the Shoe Really Fit?

Pillow: Good evening, I'm Pillow Jones and this is the Fairy Land *BTL Report*. Tonight, *BTL* investigates one of the most beloved fairy tales of all time: Cinderella. Her whole life was a fairy tale. But now, a new question arises: *Did the shoe really fit*? I'm speaking to Croolene Vutch, one of Cinderella's so-called "evil" stepsisters. What about it, Ms. Vutch? Did the shoe fit?

Croolene: No way, Pillow. No way did THAT girl's foot fit into THAT glass slipper. It just DIDN'T happen. No way.

Pillow: May I ask you how you know that, Ms. Vutch?

Croolene: I was her evil stepsister, wasn't I? You think evil stepsisters don't know these kinds of things? Of course we do!

Pillow: Next, we hear from Mike the coach driver. Mike, you were last seen driving Cinderella home from the Royal Ball in a pumpkin.

Mike: I *told* her to get back before midnight. But did she listen? No! So there I am, driving a pumpkin! The guys down at the garage—they still rib me about it.

Model

The princess's glass slipper measured 24.07 centimeters. Which of these foot measurements would fit exactly into the slipper?

24.7 $24\frac{7}{100}$ 24.007 $24\frac{70}{1000}$

First change all numbers to decimal. Then line up the numbers and compare them.

24.7 = 24.700

$24\frac{7}{100}$ = 24.070 (circled)

24.007 = 24.007

$24\frac{70}{1000}$ = 24.070 (circled)

24.07 = 24.070 (boxed)

Circle the number equal to each bold-faced number.

1. **2.4**	2.04	$2\frac{4}{10}$	$2\frac{40}{100}$	$2\frac{4}{100}$
2. **4.5**	$4\frac{5}{10}$	40.50	4.050	$4\frac{50}{100}$
3. **0.6**	$\frac{6}{10}$	0.60	0.060	$\frac{6}{100}$
4. **2.13**	2.130	$2\frac{13}{100}$	$2\frac{13}{1000}$	$2\frac{1}{300}$
5. **4.07**	4.7	4.70	$4\frac{70}{100}$	$4\frac{70}{1000}$

Ordering Fraction & Decimals

Name ______________________________ Date ______________

Pillow: What about Cinderella, Mike. Was that her slipper?

Mike: Beats me. Does it matter? I mean, she's the princess now, and I'm still drivin' this crummy PUMPKIN!

Pillow: Now, please welcome Merlin. Can you tell us what happened that night?

Merlin: After the ball, Cinderella came in complaining of foot pain. She said she'd been dancing a lot and her feet were swollen. So I gave her a foot-shrinking potion.

Pillow: Here's the big question, Merlin. Did your potion shrink her foot *beyond* its normal size? So she could fit into a glass slipper that *didn't* really belong to her?

Merlin: Wow! Maybe you're right!

Pillow: Do you realize what you're saying here, sir? The princess who calls herself Cinderella might not be the REAL Cinderella?

Sneezy: *(entering the room)* Excuse me, but this conversation is over.

Pillow: Who are you?

Sneezy: I'm Sneezy the Dwarf, attorney representing Fairy Tale Inc. My client has an interest in Stories With Happy Endings. Any information that knowingly spoils a happy ending will be shut down immediately. I'm putting a gag on this story—NOW!

Pillow: But you can't do that! This is *BTL*, Fairy Land's most popular investigative show.

Sneezy: Oh no? You just watch me. That's it everyone!

Pillow: This is Pillow Jones, signing off for the *BTL Report*. I'm—

Sneezy: Good night, everyone.

THE END

Model

Merlin made following shoe-size measurements of four different princesses in inches. Rank the measurements from small to large.

(a) 8.3 (b) 8.003 (c) $8\frac{3}{100}$ (d) $8\frac{31}{100}$

Change all numbers to decimal. Then line up the numbers and compare them.

$$8.003 = 8.003$$

$$\frac{8.3}{100} = 8.030$$

$$8.3 = 8.300$$

$$\frac{8.31}{100} = 8.310$$

The correct order is b, c, a, d.

Rank each group of numbers from smallest to largest.

6. (a) 63 (b) 0.63 (c) 6.03 (d) $6\frac{3}{10}$

_______ _______ _______ _______

7. (a) 0.42 (b) $\frac{42}{1000}$ (c) $\frac{4}{10}$ (d) $\frac{425}{1000}$

_______ _______ _______ _______

8. (a) 88.3 (b) 83.8 (c) $88\frac{31}{100}$ (d) 8.838

_______ _______ _______ _______

9. (a) $4\frac{4}{100}$ (b) 4.004 (c) $4\frac{3}{10}$ (d) $4\frac{47}{1000}$

_______ _______ _______ _______

10. (a) 9.81 (b) 9.9 (c) $9\frac{99}{100}$ (d) 9.099

_______ _______ _______ _______

Name ______________________________ Date ______________

Judy Echo and Chuck Narcissus, Part 1

Long ago, there was a fabulous movie director named Judy Echo. How fabulous was Echo? The reviews always raved.

"*Echo is fabulous*!" raved Aphrodite Smith, in the *Olympian Times*.

"*A winner*!" said Athena Cruz, of the *Delphi Oracle*.

And finally, Doug Apollo, from *Corinthian Movie Pix* wrote: "*I laughed. I cried. I also coughed, sneezed, hiccupped, wheezed, and made squirrel noises. Judy Echo is Truly Fabulous*!"

Everything was going great for Judy Echo. But then she directed a movie called *Jupiter Is a Bully*.

It wasn't that the movie was bad. In fact, if anything it was good—too *good*. Perhaps it was even too real. In the movie, Echo was not shy at all about expressing her own strong ideas about Hollywood. The movie told the story of a Hollywood studio boss, a bullying character who was a lot like real-life studio boss Hank Zeus, the CEO of Gorgon Studios. In fact, some people said the movie character was *exactly* like Zeus. And Zeus was not pleased.

Model

Judy pays $274.53 per day to rent props for her movie. How much will she pay for props over a 10-day shooting schedule? A 100-day shooting schedule? Use mental math.

$274.53 x 10 = 274.53 → $2745.30 (1 place right)

$274.53 x 100 = 274.53 → $27,453.00 (2 places right)

Move the decimal point 1 place to the right to multiply by 10.
Move the decimal point 2 places to the right to multiply by 100.
Move the decimal point 3 places to multiply by 1000. And so on.

Use mental math to multiply each number.

1. 4.6 x 10 = _______

2. 5.73 x 10 = _______

3. 0.47 x 10 = _______

4. 291.3 x 10 = _______

5. 6.4 x 100 = _______

Name ______________________ Date ____________

6. 48.55 x 100 = _______

7. 3.8 x 100 = _______

8. 427.4 x 100 = _______

9. 0.019 x 10 = _______

10. 2345.6 x 10 = _______

11. 498.4 x 100 = _______

12. 7.625 x 100 = _______

13. 4.5 x 1000 = _______

14. 29.1 x 1000 = _______

15. 2.04 x 1000 = _______

16. After her first hit, Judy Narcissus ordered a new director's chair for herself that cost 10 times as much as her old $29.74 chair. How much did the new chair cost?

____

In fact, Zeus was furious.

"Echo will never work in this town again!" thundered Zeus.

"But you can't do that, boss," Zeus's lackeys told him. "We have Echo under contract for the next nine years."

"All right then, what *can* I do?" asked the irate boss.

So it was decided. Echo would no longer be given any *good* projects. Whatever jobs she got, they would all be hack work: B-list actors, B-list scripts, cheap copies, and low-grade rip-offs.

"That'll teach Echo to mess with Zeus!" the executive roared.

And so, Judy Echo, star director, suddenly became a nobody. Nobody wanted to work with her. Nobody gave her good scripts.

"If only I could find some rising young star," she thought. Then she could become *somebody* again, a top director.

It was around this time that a "fabulous" new actor named Chuck Narcissus hit the scene. Echo desperately wanted to make a movie with Narcissus.

"Work with me!" she said to Narcissus. "I'll make you a star."

"Who are you?" he said to Echo. "You're nobody."

And it was true. By now, Echo truly was a nobody in Hollywood. She had no movies. She had no scripts. She couldn't even get anyone to *do lunch* with her anymore.

Cruel Narcissus! A single movie with Narcissus might have saved her career. But Narcissus wasn't interested.

To be continued . . .

Name ______________________ Date ______________

Judy Echo and Chuck Narcissus, Part 2

In Part 1 of our story, Hollywood director Judy Echo's outspoken ideas got her in trouble. She went from star director to *nobody* as a result of making a movie that displeased Hank Zeus, the studio boss of Gorgon Studios.

Echo dreamed of reviving her career to its old glory. And the person who would help her do that was Chuck Narcissus, a sensational young actor.

But Narcissus would have nothing to do with Echo. And so, Echo's career began to fade. For a while, she was a B-list director, working on junk scripts.

Model

Judy received a flat fee of $42,680.15 to direct a quickie movie. If she finished in 10 days, how much would she earn each day? If she finished in 100 days? Use mental math. Remember when using money units, you must round to the nearest one-hundredth.

42,680.15 ÷ 10 = 4268 0.15 → 4268.015 →
(1 place left)

(round) $4268.02

42,680.15 ÷ 100 = 426 80.15 → 426.8015 →
(2 places left)

(round) $426.80

Move the decimal point 1 place to the left to divide by 10.
Move the decimal point 2 places to the left to divide by 100.
Move the decimal point 3 places to divide by 1000. And so on.

Use mental math to divide each number.

1. 7.9 ÷ 10 = _______
2. 2.56 ÷ 10 = _______
3. 0.25 ÷ 10 = _______
4. 391.3 ÷ 10 = _______
5. 116.2 ÷ 100 = _______
6. 25.95 ÷ 100 = _______
7. 43.91 ÷ 100 = _______
8. 235.2 ÷ 100 = _______
9. 0.6 ÷ 100 = _______
10. 339.6 ÷ 10 = _______
11. 5431.2 ÷ 1000 = _______
12. 0.25 ÷ 100 = _______
13. 0.65 ÷ 1000 = _______
14. 4.672 ÷ 100 = _______
15. 28.712 ÷ 1000 = _______
16. 0.2 ÷ 1000 = _______

Mental Math: Dividing With Decimals

Name ______________________________ **Date** ______________

After falling to the C-list, and finally, without any movies to direct, she decided to try doing other things. Judy Echo tried acting, but she wasn't really any good at it. She tried stunt work with a similar result.

One day Hank Zeus was visiting a movie set when he saw a clumsy stunt person almost ruin an entire scene.

"Who is that fool?" Zeus asked.

When he was told that it was none other than Judy Echo herself, Zeus called her in to his office and offered her a job as his personal assistant.

"But why would you give me a job?" asked Echo.

"To show that I'm not such a bad guy after all," said Zeus.

Echo took the job, and she was good at it. Over time, Zeus came to rely on her for just about everything. But the more Zeus relied on Echo, the more she just faded into the background.

After a while the once-outspoken Echo seemed to have no real personality or voice of her own. Whatever Zeus said, Echo would simply repeat.

"Fabulous!" Zeus would shout.

Then Echo would repeat: "Fabulous!"

"Wonderful!" Zeus would cry.

Then Echo would repeat: "Wonderful!"

Echo, who once had been known for her strong personality, had become so shy that she didn't even show her face anymore. She became content to just stay in the background and "echo" whatever pronouncements Zeus made.

Was Echo really content just to be an assistant to the mighty Zeus, or was she simply a victim of circumstance? No one really knows for sure. What is known is that Judy Echo always kept a photo of Narcissus with her wherever she went.

As the years passed, the word "echo" became permanently connected to Judy Echo. And to this day, if you ever find yourself in the office of a movie executive, and somebody makes a statement that is followed by a low echo, keep in mind that you are listening Echo, still pining away for her beloved Narcissus, always to echo the words of others, never to express her own.

THE END

17. Script writer Toby Konopka was paid $96,235.52 for a 100-page script. Per page, how much was Toby paid?

____

18. Gorgon Studios paid $1,231,445 for 100 TV commercials. How much did each commercial cost?

____

Name ______________________________ **Date** ______________

The Royal Ninny

In the far and distant times, the Kingdom of Farkus was populated by honest, straight-forward citizens who were not afraid to speak their minds.

What a pity!

The king, you see, didn't want honest citizens who would speak their minds. He wanted someone to agree with him.

"What this kingdom needs is a true ninny," the king said. Someone with absolutely no principles or convictions, no spine or backbone. A real yes-man. Or yes-woman.

But who would step forward?

Alas, no one did. So the king sponsored a tournament to see who could win the title of Royal Ninny.

Fools came from far and wide. Twirps and slouches arrived in droves. All seeking glory.

But only one would win.

The tournament began. One by one the contestants faced off against one another. At the end of two rounds of competition the two favorites, Dora the Whiner and Jeffrey the Sniveler were dueling for the lead, both putting on a remarkable display of spineless whining and cowering.

But what was this? A third contender, known only as Richard the Puddle-Heart, suddenly surged into contention with a spectacular round of flattery and mewling. Could Puddle-Heart, as he was known, score an upset victory?

Model

In the Blabbering competition, Dora scored a 9.357 and Jeffrey scored a 9.162. Round Dora's score to the nearest 0.1 (tenths) place and Jeffrey's score to the nearest 0.01 (hundredths) place.

Step 1: Circle the place you're rounding to.

tenths	hundredths
9.(3)57	9.1(6)2

Step 2: Look to the next place to the right.
If 5 or greater, round up.
If 4 or less, round down.

round up	round down
9.3(5)7	9.16(2)

Step 3: Write each rounded number.

tenths: 9.4 **hundredths: 9.16**

Round to the tenths place.

1. 5.43 _______

2. 18.67 _______

3. 0.58 _______

4. 224.39 _______

Round to the hundredths place.

5. 485.221 _______

6. 0.433 _______

7. 2.483 _______

8. 6.0468 _______

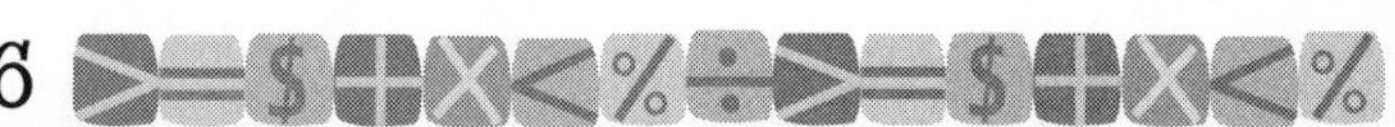

Rounding & Estimating Decimals

Name ______________________________ **Date** ______________

To determine a winner, the king asked a final question to each contestant separately:

"I have decided to award the title to one of your rivals. You yourself will be thrown in the dungeon. What do you think of my decision, my good ninny?"

Now, try as they could, neither Dora nor Jeffrey could show any happy enthusiasm for the king's decision. After all, if they did, they themselves would be thrown in the dungeon!

But Puddle-Heart was a ninny through and through.

"What a splendid idea!" Puddle-Heart said to the king. "Why didn't I think of that myself!"

At this, the king declared the competition over. Bells rang. Music played. Richard the Puddle-Heart was crowned Royal Ninny!

"He truly has the heart of a puddle," declared the king.

The audience cheered for the new Royal Ninny. The king was so happy that he didn't even throw Dora the Whiner or Jeffrey the Sniveler into the dungeon.

In fact, he named them both Assistants to the Royal Ninny, and together the three served the kingdom well as the Council of Ninnies. And they all lived happily ever after.

THE END

Model

Before the Sniveling event, Puddle-Heart had a total of 16.37 points. What was his total after receiving a score of 4.89 in Sniveling? Estimate by rounding to the nearest whole number.

6.37 → 6

4.89 → 5

6 + 5 = 11

Estimate the sums and differences.

9. 4.1 + 3.8 _______

10. 9.5 – 6.1 _______

11. 13.73 + 8.6 _______

12. 19.88 – 4.22 _______

13. 1.59 – 0.9 _______

14. 56.88 + 3.7 _______

15. 21.062 – 4.8 _______

16. 44.38 + 9.9 _______

17. In the Spinelessness competition, Dora received a score of 6.43 while Jeffrey's score was 6.39. When rounded to the nearest tenth, who received a greater score?

____

18. Puddle-Heart's total score of 38.25 was increased by 12.57 points when he agreed with the king. When rounded to the nearest whole number, what total did Puddle-Heart end up with?

____

Name ______________________ Date __________

Channel F Presents the Kissing Olympics

Pillow: Hello, and welcome to the Kissing Olympics on Channel F. I'm Pillow Jones, your host. Let's say hello to my cohost, Smoochie Wilson, former Gold Medalist in the Freestyle Olympic Liplock.

Smoochie: Hi Pillow. This is really going to be exciting. I'm stoked. I can't wait. Who's up first?

Pillow: In the Open Smooching Category our first kisser is Prince Andrei the Fair from the Kingdom of Upper Myopia. Andrei has chosen to kiss a warthog and turn it into a beautiful princess. This kiss has a degree of difficulty of 9.25.

Smoochie: Sounds tough. Hope he has his lip balm.

Pillow: Here goes Prince Andrei. He begins with a classic bow from the waist and follows it up with a full two-and-one-half cape swirl. Now he's into his approach and . . . there it is! A fine smooch, dead center. Good pop. Nice pucker. Excellent smack.

Smoochie: Actually, the Prince got a little more cheek than he would've liked. Let's see the result . . .

Model

For style, Prince Andrei received 8.563 points and 7.8 points. How many points did he receive in all?

Line up the decimal points. Attach zeroes if necessary. Then add.

$$\begin{array}{r} 8.563 \\ +\ 7.800 \\ \hline 16.363 \end{array}$$

Find each sum.

1. 4.9 + 7.34
2. 18.1 + 6.95
3. 6.24 + 11.07
4. 115.3 + 4.587
5. 2.92 + 1.38
6. 12 + 5.94
7. 19.44 + 5.68
8. 28.6 + 234.56

Adding & Subtracting Decimals

Name ______________________________ Date ______________

Pillow: Did the warthog change into a beautiful princess?

Smoochie: Not exactly, Pillow. It looks like the warthog changed into a hideous toad instead. Too bad for Prince Andrei! Better luck next time.

Pillow: Next up we have Princess Monique of Castle X. Her kiss will have a maximum degree of difficulty of 10.0. In a single smooch, she'll try to change Prince Jerkus the Younger—a spoiled, lazy, young scoundrel—into a fine young man of noble character. And here she goes . . .

Smoochie: She's trying a slanted 60-degree angle approach with a full two-and-one-half sweeping swoop.

Sound: SMACK!

Smoochie: Wow, did you hear that, Pillow? She's *some* kisser! It looks like she's taken our young prince by surprise.

Pillow: Prince Jerkus is not such a jerk anymore. He's turned into a fine young man!

Prince Jerkus: *(sincerely)* I confess: I've been a fool! I'm going to change my lazy ways! You have my noble word!

Pillow: And there it is! A complete success! And that's all we have time for. I'm Pillow Jones, speaking for Smoochie Wilson, saying so long and happy smooching, everyone!

THE END

Model

Princess Monique got just 0.053 points taken off from a perfect score of 10. What was her score?

Line up the decimal points. Attach zeroes and decimal points if necessary. Then subtract.

$$\begin{array}{r} 10.000 \\ -\ 0.053 \\ \hline 9.947 \end{array}$$

Find each difference.

9. 8.1 – 5.7

10. 16.4 – 2.91

11. 24.3 – 21.77

12. 0.59 – 0.2

13. 6 – 2.76

14. 14 – 7.065

15. 7.38 – 5

16. 12 – 0.071

17. Smoochie's Pro-Kiss Lip Balm comes in two sizes: 3.82 ounces and 5.6 ounces. How much more balm do you get in the larger tube?

____

Name ______________________________ Date ______________

The Genie and the Three Wishes

One day, a young student named Molly, who was studying to be a lawyer, bought a lamp at a garage sale and rubbed it. Out popped a genie who gave her three wishes.

"Your wish is my command," said the genie.

"All right," Molly said. "I'll wish for nice weather tomorrow."

"*Nice weather*?" said the genie. "Is that *all*?"

"Well, it's all I want right now," Molly said. "My life is going just fine, actually. I don't need any wishes. You can give them to someone else who really needs them."

"I'm sorry," said the genie. "You'll have to do that yourself."

So Molly put an ad in the paper. Soon she was getting calls from all sorts of wishers.

"I need money," said one.

"I need a giant sports utility vehicle," said another.

"I need a diamond necklace," said a third.

And so it went. Molly was about to give up when she saw a young boy with a sweet face riding his bike. His name was Mikey.

"How would you like a very special gift, Mikey?" Molly asked the boy.

Mikey's face lit up. "Oh boy!" he cried.

So Molly gave Mikey the two wishes.

"For my first wish," Mikey said, "I would like a big 6.27-ounce bag of corn chips every day."

Model

Suppose Mikey gets a 6.27 ounce bag of corn chips for 13 days. How many ounces of corn chips will he eat in all?

Step 1	Step 2	Step 3
2 6.27 x 13 1881 6270 8151	6.27 x 13 1881 6270 8151	6.27 x 13 1881 6270 81.51 ← 2 places left
Step 1: Multiply as you would with whole numbers.	**Step 2: Count the number decimal places: 2**	**Step 3: Move the decimal point to the left the same number of places.**

Find each product.

1. $\begin{array}{r} 8.12 \\ \times\ 4 \\ \hline \end{array}$

2. $\begin{array}{r} 39.75 \\ \times\ 12 \\ \hline \end{array}$

3. $\begin{array}{r} 0.89 \\ \times\ 25 \\ \hline \end{array}$

4. $\begin{array}{r} 39.75 \\ \times\ 6 \\ \hline \end{array}$

5. $\begin{array}{r} 586 \\ \times\ 1.7 \\ \hline \end{array}$

6. $\begin{array}{r} 7.079 \\ \times\ 43 \\ \hline \end{array}$

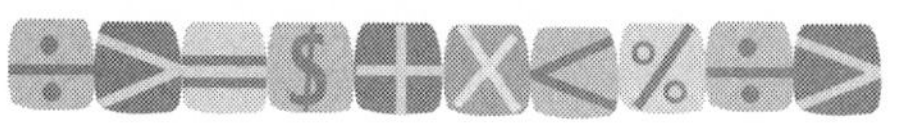

Multiplying Decimals

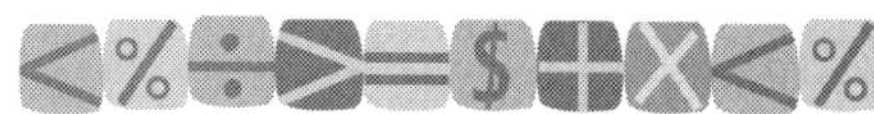

Name ______________________________ **Date** ______________

7. 126
   x 3.2

8. 0.122
   x 58

9. 532
   x 24.7

10. 32.31
    x 5865

11. 4.027
    x 52

12. 0.009
    x 78

"And for my second wish," Mikey said, "I would like to become Big Mike, all-powerful ruler of the world!"

Suddenly the entire planet was ruled by an all-powerful nine-year-old who liked corn chips.

"OBEY ME OR ELSE!" Big Mike commanded.

"Oh no!" cried Molly. "What have I done?"

She went to the genie and asked if she could get her wishes back.

"Hey, you're the lawyer," said the genie.

"I'm only a law student," Molly said. But, she finally found a way out: Mikey was only nine years old. *She had made a deal with a minor!*

Well, to make a long story short, it took awhile for the case to drag through the courts, but Molly finally won. Mikey's wish was canceled. The rule of Big Mike ended. Mikey went back to being a cute little boy.

"Thank goodness!" said Molly.

There are two morals to this story. One is: *Never give your wishes to a boy who wants to become an all-powerful dictator.* The second one is: *Make sure you get a good lawyer.*

THE END

Model

A lawyer charged $1.64 a minute for advice. How much would 445 minutes of advice cost?

Step 1	Step 2	Step 3
2 1 ~~3~~ ~~2~~ 1.64 x 445 820 6560 65600 72980	1.64 x 445 820 6560 65600 72980	1.64 x 445 820 6560 65600 7.2980 4 places left
Step 1: Multiply as you would with whole numbers.	**Step 2:** Count the number of decimal places: 4	**Step 3:** Move the decimal point to the left the same number of places.

Find each product.

13. 9.43
    x 5

14. 17.6
    x 4.3

15. 0.97
    x 0.6

16. 554.9
    x 2.8

17. 6.98
    x 4.6

18. 6.067
    x 0.51

Name ______________________ Date ____________

The Baa Baa Report

Fairy Land's Eyewitness Crime Report

Reported by Baa Baa Black Sheep

Fairy Land—Baa Baa leads off today with shocking news. Old Mother Hubbard—the well-known Fairy Land society figure—is alleged to have visited her cupboard on May 3 at 9:03 A.M. Why? The police report clearly states that she went there for one reason only: she wanted to quote "get her poor dog a bone." But when she got there, things suddenly turn ugly: *the cupboard was bare*!

So the poor dog got none.

Now here's where the story gets interesting: Why was Mother Hubbard's cupboard bare? Evidence points to a nefarious underworld character known only as the Crooked Man, who allegedly "bought a crooked cat, which caught a crooked mouse, and they all lived together in a crooked little house." Now, if that doesn't sound a bit "bent" to you, then you're just not paying attention.

Model

Dog Bone snack treats come in a 21.36 ounce bag. Each bag contains 8 bones. How much does each bone weigh?

$8\overline{)21.36}$

Step 1: Bring the decimal point straight up.

$$\begin{array}{r} 2.67 \\ 8\overline{)21.36} \\ -16 \\ \hline 53 \\ -48 \\ \hline 56 \\ -56 \\ \hline 0 \end{array}$$

Step 2: Divide. Leave the decimal point in place.

Find each quotient.

1. $4\overline{)13.6}$
2. $3\overline{)23.7}$
3. $5\overline{)41.5}$
4. $6\overline{)34.2}$
5. $8\overline{)130.4}$
6. $7\overline{)185.5}$
7. $14\overline{)78.4}$
8. $47\overline{)766.1}$
9. $26\overline{)111.8}$
10. $8\overline{)188.56}$

Name ______________________________ Date ______________

On the other hand, we have another suspect named Jack. But here, things get murky. Is it Jack B. Nimble or Jack B. Quick? And what about the Jack who jumped over the candlestick? That's not to mention Little Jack Horner, who claims all he did was sit in a corner, but as far as Baa Baa is concerned, Horner could still be guilty.

As you can see, the list just keeps growing. Which brings us back to Old Mother Hubbard herself. She's a familiar figure, but how well do we really know her?

Sources say that Mother Hubbard is not really old (she's 36), not really a mother (she lives with her dog), and doesn't really even own a cupboard (she lives in Mother Goose Motor Inn Motel).

So where does that leave us? I'm afraid Ol' Baa Baa's going to have to take a raincheck on that one, folks because at this point the Mother Hubbard Caper is still a wide-open case.

THE END

Model

Jack B. Nimble ran 23 yards in 4 seconds. At this rate, how many yards did he run in 1 second?

$$4\overline{)23.}$$

$$\begin{array}{r} 5. \\ 4\overline{)23.} \\ -20 \end{array} \qquad \begin{array}{r} 5.7 \\ 4\overline{)23.0} \\ -20 \\ 3\,0 \\ -2\,8 \\ 2 \end{array} \qquad \begin{array}{r} 5.75 \\ 4\overline{)23.00} \\ -20 \\ 3\,0 \\ -2\,8 \\ 20 \\ -20 \\ 0 \end{array}$$

Step 1: Write in a decimal point. Then bring it up.

Step 2: Begin dividing.

Step 3: Attach zeroes if they are needed.

Step 4: Finish dividing.

Find each quotient.

11. $2\overline{)15}$

12. $4\overline{)37}$

13. $6\overline{)51}$

14. $5\overline{)24}$

15. $8\overline{)12}$

16. $5\overline{)3}$

17. $8\overline{)11}$

18. $50\overline{)20}$

19. $60\overline{)3}$

20. $20\overline{)4}$

21. $16\overline{)408}$

22. $28\overline{)175}$

Name ______________________ Date ____________

The Quest for the Holly Gray-L

Not such a long time ago a computer genius named Holly Gray invented a computer program that could tell jokes. And not just any jokes, either. These jokes were so funny they even made *computers* laugh!

She called this program the Holly Gray-L. (the "L" was for "Laughs.")

Well, there was a big to-do about this program. Then suddenly Holly disappeared for three weeks. And she took the Holly Gray-L program with her.

No one could find Holly or the Holly Gray-L. So Holly's company, Medieval Chalice Computers or MCC, sponsored a competition to see who could find a new joke-telling program.

The Quest for the new Holly Gray-L was on!

Model

The Holly Gray-L told 14 jokes in 9 minutes. What was the rate of joke-telling in jokes per minute?

Step 1: Divide as you would normally.

Step 2: Round off the quotient of the repeating decimal to the nearest hundredth.

$1.555... = 1.\overline{5}$ or 1.56

```
  1.555...
9|14.00
  9
  50
 -45
   50
  -45
    5
```

The line shows a repeating decimal: $1.\overline{5} = 1.55555...$

Find each quotient. Round to the nearest hundredth.

1. $3\overline{)4}$
2. $9\overline{)20}$
3. $6\overline{)23}$
4. $9\overline{)24}$
5. $12\overline{)146}$
6. $30\overline{)170}$
7. $6\overline{)200}$
8. $60\overline{)512}$
9. $54\overline{)153}$
10. $72\overline{)208}$

Three young "knights" took up the challenge. First up was Chuck "Red" Bunsen. He punched in his "Red Knight" program and out came the joke: *Which room has no walls, ceiling, floors, or windows? Answer: a mushroom!*

Well, the computers loved this joke. They printed out HAR HAR HAR! and YUK YUK on their screens. But the humans barely cracked a smile.

Next up was Mindy Greene, whose "Green Knight" program said: *Knock, knock. Who's there? Weirdo. Weirdo who? Weirdo you think you're going, mister?*

This joke caused the human audience to laugh like crazy, but the computers didn't get it, possibly because they didn't understand the "weirdo" spelling.

Rounding Decimal Quotients

Name ______________________________ Date ____________

Finally there was a knight named Yarg of Ylloh. Yarg's "Gray Knight" program told a joke that was so funny that smoke and sparks started coming out of the computers. Then they burst into flames.

At this point, Yarg took off her disguise to reveal that she was none other than the missing Holly Gray ("Yarg Ylloh" spelled backwards!) and that her program was the Holly Gray-L itself!

"Let's hear Holly's joke!" the audience cried.

"I can't risk it," Holly said. "The joke is just TOO funny. Once you hear it, you CANNOT STOP LAUGHING. I myself laughed for three straight weeks."

"How did you ever stop?" audience members asked.

"Reality TV shows," Holly said. "They were so boring that I stopped laughing almost immediately. In fact," Holly added, "I haven't laughed since!"

One thing was clear. The Quest for the Holly Gray-L was over. The thing was just too darn funny.

THE END

Model

An audience of 11 computers gave the Green Knight's joke a total score of 24 points. What was the average score?

Step 1: Divide 24 by 11.

Step 2: Round to the nearest hundredth.

```
       2.1818... = 2.18
  11 | 24.0000
     - 22
        20
       -11
         90
        -88
          20
         -11
          90
```

____

Find each quotient.

11. $7\overline{)39}$

12. $13\overline{)60}$

13. $14\overline{)128}$

14. $19\overline{)249}$

15. $7\overline{)52.4}$

16. $23\overline{)84.6}$

17. $13\overline{)444.4}$

18. $29\overline{)824.63}$

19. To replace the Holly Gray-L, Holly invented the Joke Machine. The Joke Machine churned out 73 jokes in 15 seconds. How many jokes per second did the Joke Machine create?

____

20. To rate jokes, Holly created the Humor Quotient (HQ). To find a joke's Humor Quotient, divide the number of audience members who laugh by the number who do not laugh. What is the HQ for a joke that made 57 people laugh and 18 people not laugh?

____

Fractured Fairy Tales: Fractions & Decimals • Scholastic Teaching Resources

Name ______________________ Date ______________

The Fairy Tale World's Greatest Newspaper

★ THE FRACTURED ★ FAIRY TALE GAZETTE

VOL. CLIII . . . . No. 55,554 Monday, September 24 $3.00

Wolf Guarding Henhouse to Resign

A *Gazette* Exclusive

by Hilton Wolfe, Former Henhouse Guard

My name is Hilton Wolfe. I'm a guard at the henhouse. Or at least I was until I was fired by Farmer Brown last week.

I know what you're thinking. *A wolf guarding a henhouse.* Not such a hot idea. Well perhaps not.

But consider this. I was hired by Farmer Brown himself. I've been working at this henhouse for over three years now. And chicken attacks are down over 43 percent. Forty-three percent! You think that's a coincidence? I don't.

Model

What does 43% mean?

$43\% = \frac{43}{100}$

$43\% = 0.43$

$43\% = 43$ out of 100

Write each percent as a decimal.

1. 31% ______
2. 90% ______
3. 25% ______
4. 46% ______
5. 9% ______
6. 52.6% ______
7. 3.7% ______
8. 80.3% ______

Write each percent as a fraction.

9. 22% ______
10. 97% ______
11. 3% ______
12. 57% ______

Write each decimal or fraction as a percent.

13. 0.19 ______
14. $\frac{13}{100}$ ______
15. 0.55 ______
16. $\frac{24}{100}$ ______
17. $\frac{77}{100}$ ______
18. $\frac{5}{100}$ ______
19. 0.06 ______
20. 0.67 ______

Percents

Name ______________________________ **Date** ______________

The Fractured Fairy Tale Gazette — page 2

Now ask yourself, *Why would Farmer Brown hire a wolf to guard the henhouse in the first place?*

Well, I put in for the job just like anyone else. I saw the ad on the barnyard door. I sent in my resumé. I never let my background or personal feelings get in the way of how I perform my job.

I'm a professional.

And most importantly, *I never once tried to cover up my true identity.* I'm a wolf—and proud of it. We wolves actually have a long history of guarding henhouses. Sure, we've sometimes been known to have a few run-ins with the chickens.

But who hasn't?

Having worked in a henhouse for over three years, I can tell you, firsthand—chickens are no picnic. They're noisy, loud, dirty, bothersome, obnoxious creatures.

Hey, I know what you're thinking. *Why should we believe a wolf?* Well, I agree. Don't take my word for it. Go ask the chickens what they think. They'll tell you what I was like.

I was fair and honest 99 percent of the time. And none of the chickens got away. And that's about all you can ask for when it comes to guarding a henhouse.

THE END

Model

What does 99 percent of the time mean?

$$99\% = \frac{99}{100} \rightarrow \text{almost all of the time}$$

Match each percent to a phrase.

21. 100% _______ a. almost never

22. 50% _______ b. sometimes

23. 1% _______ c. never

24. 51% _______ d. all of the time

25. 10% _______ e. rarely

26. 30% _______ f. half of the time

27. 0% _______ g. a majority of the time

28. As a fraction, 50% = _______/100

Simplify the fraction: _______.

1/2 is the same as _______%.

29. As a fraction, 10% = _______/100

Simplify the fraction: _______.

1/10 is the same as _______%.

30. As a fraction, 25% = ___/100

Simplify the fraction: _____.

1/4 is the same as ____ %.

Name ______________________________ Date ______________

Great Hero and Total Coward

Each year the Mice held a Grand Council meeting and each year they decided the exact same thing: they should put a bell on the cat. The trouble was, no one would do it. It took great courage to bell a cat. And mice, in general, were not a very courageous group.

One year, two newcomers came to the meeting. One had the very curious name of Great Hero. The other was called Total Coward. When the call went up for volunteers to put a bell on the cat, a voice suddenly spoke up from the back.

"I can do that," said the voice.

"Who are you?" asked the Council leader.

"I am called Total Coward," she said.

"I'm sorry," the Council leader said. "This is not a job for a total coward. Is anyone here a great hero?"

Great Hero stood. "I am Great Hero," he said.

"Then it is done," the leader said. "You will put the bell on the cat. And we will all finally be free of fear."

"B-but—," began Great Hero.

Model

In the Council, 0.86 of the mice were cowards. What percent were cowards?

0.86 x 100 = 86%

Only $\frac{1}{5}$ of the Council leaders felt that Total Coward could do the job. What percent is this?

1 out of 5 = $\frac{1}{5} \rightarrow 5\overline{)1.0}$ = 20% (quotient: 0.2)

Change each quantity to percent.

1. 0.63 ______
2. $\frac{3}{10}$ ______
3. 0.55 ______
4. $\frac{1}{4}$ ______
5. $\frac{1}{2}$ ______
6. 0.2 ______
7. $\frac{3}{5}$ ______
8. 0.33 ______
9. 0.06 ______
10. $\frac{7}{20}$ ______
11. 0.74 ______
12. $\frac{9}{25}$ ______
13. $\frac{5}{8}$ ______
14. 0.993 ______
15. $\frac{1}{20}$ ______
16. 0.025 ______

Fractions, Decimals & Percents

Name ______________________________ **Date** ______________

The trouble was, Great Hero was not very much of a hero. In fact, Great Hero was pretty much a coward. Total Coward, on the other hand, was quite brave.

"Don't worry," Total Coward told Great Hero. "We'll find a way to get the job done."

They took the bell and approached the Cat.

"Who are you?" asked the cat.

"I'm Total Coward," said Total Coward.

"I can see that," said the Cat. "And I hate cowards—the way they squeal and beg. They're not even any fun to catch."

"I agree," said Total Coward. "And that's why I'm here. As a Total Coward, it is my duty to present you with our Enemy of the Year Award."

"Aw," gushed the Cat, "You shouldn't have. What an honor!"

"My friend Great Hero here has the trophy for you," said Total Coward. And she pointed over the Great Hero, who was quivering with fear, holding the bell.

"*That's* your Great Hero?" said the cat. "He looks like a total coward to me. And that trophy looks a lot like a bell."

"Oh, I assure you this is a fine trophy," said Total Coward. "Why don't you try it on?"

So the cat tried on the "trophy," and that was how Great Hero and Total Coward belled the cat. Once the bell was safely fastened around the cat's neck, the two mice scurried away. They had proven that they were not cowards, but neither were they fools.

THE END

Model

After the cat was belled, cat trouble went down by 89%. What is this percentage as a decimal and a fraction?

$$89\% \div 100 = 0.89 \rightarrow 0.89 = \frac{89}{100}$$

Complete the table.

Fraction	Decimal	Percent
$\frac{1}{10}$		10%
$\frac{1}{2}$	0.5	
	0.15	15%
$\frac{7}{10}$		
	0.29	
		71%
$\frac{2}{5}$		
		60%
	0.09	
		6%
$\frac{3}{8}$		
	0.025	
$\frac{1}{50}$		
	1.3	
		72.3%

Name ______________________ Date ____________

Why Owl Is Wise

A long time ago, the Wise Owl was thought to be no more wise than any of the other animals. He was said to be of merely average wisdom, as judged by the standards of the forest.

Along came a new Superintendent of the Forest.

"Wisdom is my top priority!" he declared.

This meant a thorough evaluation for every animal in the forest. Each creature was given a Wisdom Test to see where he or she stood.

The animals lined up for the test—Squirrel, Earthworm, Honeybee, Sparrow, Toad, Snail, and so on. And each animal needed to show how well it understood the ways of the forest.

The trouble was that different animals understood things in different ways.

"Where is the best place to dig a burrow?" asked the Superintendent.

"I don't dig burrows," Owl said.

"What is the fastest way to climb a tree?" the Superintendent asked.

"I don't climb trees," Owl said.

"Which seeds are best for eating?" the Superintendent asked.

"I don't eat seeds," Owl said, and then added, "Why don't you ask us about things we know?"

Model

In the burrowing part of the test, Owl got 7 out of 10 questions wrong. What percent did he get wrong?

7 out of 10 = $\frac{7}{10} \rightarrow \frac{7 \times 10}{10 \times 10} = \frac{70}{100}$ = 70% wrong

↑ Denominator of 100

Use an equivalent fraction with a denominator of 100 to find each percent.

1. 3 out of 10 = $\frac{3}{10} \rightarrow \frac{3 \times ?}{10 \times ?} = \frac{?}{100}$ = ______%

2. 5 out of 10 = $\frac{5}{10} \rightarrow \frac{5 \times ?}{10 \times ?} = \frac{?}{100}$ = ______%

3. 1 out of 4 = $\frac{1}{4} \rightarrow \frac{1 \times ?}{4 \times 25} = \frac{?}{100}$ = ______%

4. 3 out of 4 = $\frac{?}{?} \rightarrow \frac{? \times ?}{? \times ?} = \frac{?}{100}$ = ______%

5. 2 out of 4 = $\frac{?}{?} \rightarrow \frac{? \times ?}{? \times ?} = \frac{?}{100}$ = ______%

6. 1 out of 5 = $\frac{?}{?} \rightarrow \frac{? \times ?}{? \times ?} = \frac{?}{100}$ = ______%

Finding Percents

Name ______________________ **Date** ______________

Indeed, almost all of the questions seemed silly—at least for an owl. Then Owl got his test scores back.

"Frankly I'm disappointed," the Superintendent told him. Indeed, Owl's wisdom score put him somewhere between a Beaver and a Woodpecker.

"*Woodpecker!*" Owl fumed. "I'm no smarter than that pecking fool? Impossible!"

"I'm afraid it's true," the Superintendent said.

Over time, the bitter truth began to sink in. Unless Owl changed, his wisdom would never exceed that of a woodpecker, a creature that knocked its head against a tree all day.

So Owl took action. He went to Toad and learned where to dig burrows. He went to Squirrel and learned how to climb a tree. He went to Sparrow and learned which seeds were best for eating.

When he retook the test, Owl did splendidly. Indeed the Superintendent deemed him the "wisest animal in the forest."

"It's not true," other animals, such as Beaver, complained. "All Owl did was prepare better than the rest of us."

"Perhaps better preparation *is* a form of wisdom," the Superintendent said.

"In any event, Owl certainly never complains about his reputation for being "wise."

Even if it isn't all that true.

THE END

Model

On his second test, Owl got 4 out of 5 seed questions right. What percent did he get right?

$$4 \text{ out of } 5 = \frac{4}{5} \rightarrow 5\overline{)4.0}^{\,0.8} = 80\%$$

Use an equivalent fraction to find each percent.

7. 1 out of 2 = _______ %

8. 3 out of 5 = _______ %

9. 2 out of 8 = _______ %

10. 1 out of 8 = _______ %

11. 2 out of 5 = _______ %

12. 7 out of 20 = _______ %

13. 3 out of 8 = _______ %

14. 9 out of 12 = _______ %

15. 12 out of 15 = _______ %

Name ______________________ Date ______________

Milton Bisk, Real Estate Agent to the Stars

My name is Milton Bisk. I'm a real estate agent. I sell houses to the stars—movie stars, that is. You know, like Zeke Slunk. I sold Zeke a beach house after he won his Oscar last year.

Nice guy.

I sold Marilyn Coca-Mocha her place too, a split level with a cocoa-bean shaped pool. Lovely. And Mañana—do you like Mañana? Everybody likes Mañana! I sold her a colonial last month with five—count 'em—five kitchens!

"It's a beautiful house," I told her. "When do you plan to move in?"

"Mañana!" she told me. What a *star*!

But the deal I wanted to talk about today did not involve a beautiful star, or for that matter, even a beautiful house. In fact, we agents have a name for this kind of a property. We call it "a dump."

But no matter. This guy named Phil calls me, says he's got a property with three houses on it. One house is made of straw; one is made of twigs; and the third is made of brick.

Now a brick house I can sell. But *straw*? *Twigs*? Who would buy those?

"Don't worry," Phil insists, "there are customers out there."

Model

Milton Bisk gets a 4% commission for selling a $7500 house. How much is his commission?

$$4\% = 0.04 \rightarrow 7500 \times 0.04 = \$300$$

↑ Change to decimal

Use an equivalent fraction with a denominator of 100 to find each percent.

1. 4% of $300 = __________
2. 10% of $250 = __________
3. 25% of $2800 = __________
4. 8% of $2400 = __________
5. 90% of $700 = __________
6. 13% of $150 = __________
7. 45% of $90,000 = __________
8. 3% of $420 = __________
9. 12.5% of $800 = __________
10. 82% of $145 = __________

Name ______________________________ Date ______________

And sure enough, the next week I get a call from three brothers. The Three Pigs, they call themselves.

"What are you, some kind of musical group?" I ask.

"No," they say. "We're talent agents." For some variety act I've never heard of: A guy named Wolf who blows houses down.

"Blows houses down?" I say.

"Never mind," they say. "Just show us the houses." So I show them.

"Perfect!" they say.

So I'm sitting there thinking: *I just sold three of the WORST houses I've ever seen before.* But the Three Pigs are happy. By the next week they're staging a major media event.

BIG BAD WOLF TO BLOW DOWN 3 HOUSES! says the ad.

It takes place the following week. Wolf actually *does* blow down two of the houses. (Guess which ones?) But the third—the *brick* house—by the time he gets there, the cops move in and haul them all away for "staging a public event without a permit."

Or some such thing.

But Wolf and the Pigs got what they wanted: exposure. Sure enough, the next day it's all over the TV and the newspapers. BIG BLOW-DOWN TOMORROW where Wolf will finish the job by blowing down the house made of brick.

But the only way to see him do it is to pony up $29.95 on Pay-4-TV. I mean, $29.95 to see a wolf try to blow down a house? What is this world coming to?

But of course, that's only the opinion of one person—me, Milton Bisk, real estate agent to the stars. I may sell houses to the stars, but when it comes to understanding them, I'm just as much in the dark as everyone else.

THE END

11. Milton Bisk sold the straw house for $800. If he gets a 4% commission, how much will his commission be?

____

12. Bisk sold 60 houses this summer. Five percent of those houses were sold to pigs. How many pigs bought their house from Bisk?

____

13. Bisk got a 6% commission on a $120,000 house, and a 5% commission on a $150,000 house. Which commission was greater? By how much?

____

14. The Three Pigs get 20% of the take from the "Big Blow-Down." How much do they make on each $29.95 subscriber?

____

15. Suppose 900 people pay $29.95 each for the Big Blow-Down. If the pigs get 20% of this money, how much will they get all together? How much will each pig get?

____

16. The Wolf gets 70% of the money from problem 15 above. How much will the Wolf make?

____

17. Suppose the Wolf spends 40% of the money he made in problem 16 on a new "Wolf-Mobile" car. How much will the car cost him?

____

Name ______________________ Date ____________

Fairy Land Annual Poll

Fairy Land Dot Com wants to know what YOU think. What are your favorite fairy tales? What kinds of stories do like best? Help us find out by answering the questions below.

BEGINNINGS
Your favorite fairy tale begins with the phrase:

- ❒ Once upon a time . . .
- ❒ It was a dark and stormy night . . .
- ❒ Good evening, ladies and germs . . .
- ❒ Knock, knock. Who's there?

HEROES
Your favorite fairy tale hero is:

- ❒ a handsome young prince.
- ❒ a sniveling weasel.
- ❒ a guy named Chuck who works at the supermarket.
- ❒ a bowl of oatmeal mush.

HEROINES
Your favorite fairy tale heroine is:

- ❒ a beautiful princess with a glass slipper.
- ❒ a toad who's really a beautiful princess.
- ❒ a beautiful princess who's really an actress.
- ❒ a toad who's really a toad.

STORYLINE
Your favorite fairy tale plot is:

- ❒ an evil witch turns a handsome prince into a frog.
- ❒ a clever genie turns a princess into an old bicycle seat.
- ❒ a donkey runs for president.
- ❒ a young girl gets a job at a clothing store and works her way up to become a top-notch model who takes the fashion world by storm, only to be done in by an evil queen who turns her into an old bicycle seat.

VILLAINS
Your favorite fairy tale villain is:

- ❒ an evil queen.
- ❒ a vicious chipmunk.
- ❒ a fish named Murray.
- ❒ a plate of spaghetti and meatballs.

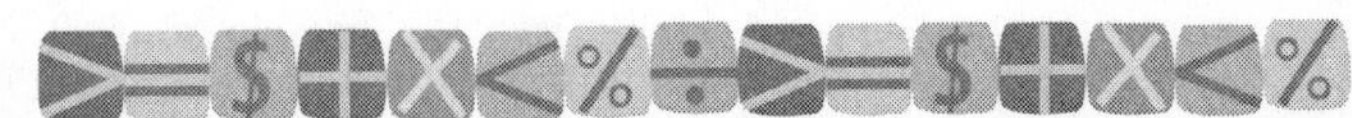

Percent Problems

Name ______________________ Date __________

CLIMAX

Your favorite fairy tale climax is:

❐ a sword fight between the hero and the villain.

❐ a Scrabble game between the hero and a chicken.

❐ the prince marries the fish after all.

❐ everyone falls asleep.

ENDINGS

Your favorite fairy tale ending is:

❐ And they lived happily ever after.

❐ And they lived happily for a while until they got sick of each other.

❐ And they all went out for a pizza.

❐ And the king had everyone thrown into the dungeon.

MORALS

Your favorite fairy tale moral is:

❐ There's no place like home.

❐ Sticks and stones may break my bones, but the truth will never hurt me.

❐ Evil sorcerers shouldn't turn princesses into frogs because they'll end up being kissed by a handsome prince in the end anyway.

❐ Don't mess with a vicious chipmunk.

1. In a book of 60 fairy tales, 90% of the stories end up with everyone living happily ever after. How many stories end happily?

   ____

2. In 60 stories, 80% of heroes were handsome. If each story had 1 hero, how many heroes were handsome?

   ____

3. In the book of fairy tales in problem 2, only 24 heroes end up marrying a fish. What percent do NOT marry a fish?

   ____

4. Some 56% of the 400 people in the Fairy Land poll were afraid of vicious chimpmunks. How many people were afraid?

   ____

5. Thirty percent of the 400 people in the poll thought "getting pizza" was the best story ending. Of these people, 75% liked pepperoni pizza. How many liked pepperoni pizza?

   ____

6. Five hundred people were asked, "Would you wear glass slippers?" There were 125 who said "Yes" and 175 who said "No." The rest said "Maybe." What percent said "Maybe"?

   ____

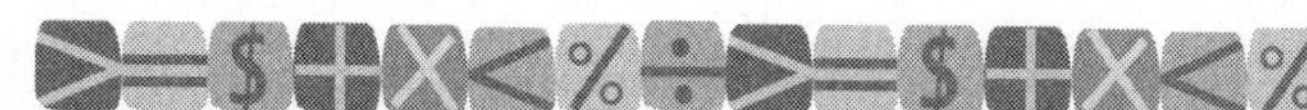

Name ______________________ Date ______________

The Fairy Tale World's Greatest Newspaper

★ THE FRACTURED ★ FAIRY TALE GAZETTE

VOL. CLIII . . . . No. 55,554 Monday, September 24 $3.00

Wicked Witch Of The South to Retire!

The Castle—In a stirring ceremony, Grinda, the Wicked Witch of the South, retired today to a resort community where she plans to garden, write, play tennis, and cast nasty spells on people who happen to get in her way.

"It's been a long haul," said Grinda. "I've done a lot of foul and wicked things in my career. Now it's time to let someone else take over."

Long ignored while her more famous sister, the Wicked Witch of the West, grabbed all the headlines, Grinda has nevertheless had her moments.

"Grinda was fond of turning people into toads and monkeys," said reporter Mary Mary Quite Contrary. "She once cast a spell on an entire *village*, giving everyone bad hair days, all on the same morning."

"She will be missed," said Rhonda, the Wicked Witch of the Northeast. "She did some truly cruel and hideous things in her day. People like that don't come along very often."

Model

In a single week, 21 out of the 28 spells cast by Grinda turned people into toads or monkeys. What percent was this?

Use a proportion: $\frac{21}{28} = \frac{n}{100}$

Cross multiply: $\frac{21}{28} \times \frac{n}{100} \rightarrow 28n = 21 \bullet 100$

Divide both sides of the equation to solve for n.

$\frac{28n}{28} = \frac{21 \bullet 100}{28} \rightarrow n = 75$

Solve the proportions.

1. $\frac{2}{5} = \frac{n}{100} =$ ____________

2. $\frac{4}{8} = \frac{n}{100} =$ ____________

3. $\frac{5}{20} = \frac{n}{100} =$ ____________

4. $\frac{8}{20} = \frac{n}{100} =$ ____________

Solving Problems With Proportions

Name ______________________ Date ____________

5. $\frac{9}{15} = \frac{n}{100} =$ ______

6. $\frac{n}{8} = \frac{50}{100} =$ ______

7. $\frac{n}{25} = \frac{20}{100} =$ ______

8. $\frac{7}{25} = \frac{n}{100} =$ ______

9. $\frac{n}{40} = \frac{60}{100} =$ ______

10. $\frac{n}{48} = \frac{75}{100} =$ ______

11. $\frac{45}{n} = \frac{90}{100} =$ ______

12. $\frac{9}{24} = \frac{21}{n} =$ ______

Even Grinda's enemies seemed to join in the celebration for this loathsome hag.

"Hey, I can't say that I *ever* liked her," said the Beautiful Princess of the castle. "But I did come to respect her. Especially when she turned my fiancée into a newt."

"You may not have always agreed with her," said Glinda, the Good Witch of the North. "But you did know where she stood: on the side of whatever was wicked and bad."

After the ceremony Grinda was asked, "What now?"

Home will be the Dark Chamber, a Modern Retirement Community Center for witches, goblins, demons, fiends, and other evil beings.

"It'll be great to be around folks like that," Grinda said. "I'm looking forward to it."

When asked whether she would retire from evil deeds altogether, Grinda said:

"As far as turning people into toads and rats, I don't think I'll do much of that any-more. It takes too much work."

But would Grinda drop her old ways completely?

This correspondent learned the answer to that question when a man cut in front of Grinda at the salad bar. Suddenly, what had been a fellow in shorts and a tank top standing in front of me was now a pink squealing pig!

And all I could say was "Oh Grinda! You rascal you!"

THE END

13. Grinda turned 60 people into newts. Forty-five of these people were princes. What percent were princes?

____

14. Grinda received 240 out of 320 votes to get in the Witch's Hall of Fame. What percent of the vote did she receive?

____

pages 8–9

1. 2/4 or 1/2
2. 2/4 or 1/2
3. 3/8
4. 5/8
5. 6/7
6. 1/7
7. ○●●●
8. ○○○○●●●

pages 10–11

1. 1/2
2. 1/3
3. 1/3
4. 1/2
5. 1/3
6. 3/4
7. 2/3
8. 2/3
9. 3/4
10. 4/5
11. 1/2
12. 1/4
13. 3/4
14. 2/3
15. 2/5
16. 5/6
17. 2/3
18. 2/5
19. 2/5
20. 3/7

pages 12–13

1. 4/3 = 1 1/3
2. 3/5
3. 4/4 = 1
4. 2/7
5. 13/9 = 1 4/9
6. 6/6 = 1
7. 2/11
8. 9/15 = 3/5
9. 6/5 = 1 1/5
10. 15/13 = 1 2/13
11. 24/17 = 1 7/17
12. 4/9
13. 6/4 = 1 2/4 = 1 1/2
14. 4/8 = 1/2
15. 10/6 = 1 4/6 = 1 2/3
16. 3/9 = 1/3

pages 14–15

1. 5/4
2. 8/3
3. 16/5
4. 29/6
5. 25/7
6. 41/8
7. 29/3
8. 99/8
9. 1 1/2
10. 1 1/4
11. 2 1/3
12. 2 1/4
13. 3 1/3
14. 2 6/7
15. 6 1/4
16. 1 2/13
17. 4 6/11
18. 4 8/23

pages 16–17

1. 6
2. 4
3. 15
4. 8
5. 5/6
6. 11/12
7. 23/24
8. 7/8
9. 7/18
10. 5/42
11. 17/20 mile
12. 1/4 foot
13. 29/40 of the day
14. 6/35 longer

pages 18–19

1. 5 11/15
2. 6
3. 9 1/20
4. 10 3/8
5. 1 11/45
6. 8 1/10
7. 16 1/24
8. 3 1/3
9. 1 7/24 minutes
10. 3 9/40 hours
11. 33 7/8 inches
12. 13 19/24 inches

pages 20–21

1. 1 1/2
2. 2 3/8
3. 3 3/4
4. 3 1/4
5. 2 4/9
6. 8 1/5
7. 6 3/8
8. 2 8/15
9. 1 2/3
10. 1 1/2
11. 1 7/10
12. 7 1/2

pages 22–23

1. 5
2. 5
3. 14
4. 3
5. 9
6. 18
7. 30
8. 12
9. 2/7
10. 10/27
11. 2/21
12. 2/9
13. 4/9
14. 2/15
15. 2/9
16. 3/20
17. 5/9
18. 3/20

pages 24–25

1. 5
2. 14
3. 36
4. 14
5. 3 1/2
6. 16 1/2
7. 4
8. 1 2/3
9. 15
10. 10
11. 3
12. 1 1/3
13. 14
14. 8
15. 3
16. 19 3/5
17. 2 4/5 ounces

pages 26–27

1. 1/3
2. 1/4
3. 2 1/2
4. 3/5
5. 3/7
6. 5/9
7. 1 3/5
8. 5/14
9. 3 3/5
10. 1 1/2
11. 2
12. 1 1/2
13. 2 1/4
14. 4/7
15. 9/10
16. 1 1/3
17. 18 dumplings
18. 6 bowls

pages 28–29

1. 6/10
2. 1 4/10
3. 2/10
4. 8 3/10
5. 14/100
6. 2 65/100
7. 37/100
8. 28 59/100
9. 3/100
10. 2 4/1000
11. 583 46/1000
12. 76/1000
13. 0.5
14. 4.4
15. 0.24
16. 6.3
17. 0.04
18. 13.45
19. 9.006
20. 241.03
21. 0.018
22. 2.41
23. 376.037
24. 82.001

pages 30–31

1. 2 4/10 and 2 40/100
2. 4 5/10 and 4 50/100
3. 6/10 and 0.60
4. 2.130 and 2 13/100
5. 4 70/1000
6. b, c, d, a
7. b, c, a, d
8. d, b, a, c
9. b, a, d, c
10. d, a, b, c

pages 32–33

1. 46
2. 57.3
3. 4.7
4. 2913
5. 640
6. 4855
7. 380
8. 42,740
9. 0.19
10. 23,456
11. 49,840
12. 762.5
13. 4500
14. 29,100
15. 2040
16. $297.40

pages 34–35

1. 0.79
2. 0.256
3. 0.025
4. 39.13
5. 1.162
6. 0.2595
7. 0.4391
8. 2.352
9. 0.006
10. 33.96
11. 5.4312
12. 0.0025
13. 0.00065
14. 0.04672
15. 0.028712
16. 0.0002
17. 962.3553, round to $962.36 per page
18. $12,314.45 per commercial

pages 36–37

1. 5.4
2. 18.7
3. 0.6
4. 224.4
5. 485.22
6. 0.43
7. 2.48
8. 6.05
9. 8
10. 4
11. 23
12. 16
13. 1
14. 61
15. 16
16. 54
17. When rounded to the nearest tenth they are the same.
18. 51

pages 38–39

1. 12.24
2. 25.05
3. 17.31
4. 119.887
5. 4.3
6. 17.94
7. 25.12
8. 263.16
9. 2.4
10. 13.49
11. 2.53
12. 0.39
13. 3.24
14. 6.935
15. 2.38
16. 11.929
17. 1.78 ounces

pages 40–41

1. 32.48
2. 477.00 or 477
3. 22.25
4. 238.5
5. 996.2
6. 304.397
7. 403.2
8. 7.076
9. 13,140.4
10. 2100.15
11. 209.404
12. 0.702
13. 47.15
14. 75.68
15. 0.582
16. 1553.72
17. 32.108
18. 3.09417

pages 42–43

1. 3.4
2. 7.9
3. 8.3
4. 5.7
5. 16.3
6. 26.5
7. 5.6
8. 16.3
9. 4.3
10. 23.57
11. 7.5
12. 9.25
13. 8.5
14. 4.8
15. 1.5
16. 0.6
17. 1.375
18. 0.4
19. 0.05
20. 0.2
21. 25.5
22. 6.25

pages 44–45

1. $1.\overline{3}$ or 1.33
2. $2.\overline{2}$ or 2.22
3. $3.8\overline{3}$ or 3.83
4. $2.\overline{6}$ or 2.67
5. $12.1\overline{6}$ or 12.17
6. $5.\overline{6}$ or 5.67
7. $33.\overline{3}$ or 33.33
8. $8.5\overline{3}$ or 8.53
9. $2.8\overline{3}$ or 2.83
10. $2.\overline{8}$ or 2.89
11. 5.57
12. 4.62
13. 9.14
14. 13.11
15. 7.49
16. 3.68
17. 34.18
18. 28.44
19. 4.87 jokes per second
20. 3.17

pages 46–47

1. 0.31
2. 0.90 or 0.9
3. 0.25
4. 0.46
5. 0.09
6. 0.526
7. 0.037
8. 0.803
9. 22/100 or 11/50
10. 97/100
11. 3/100
12. 57/100
13. 19%
14. 13%
15. 55%
16. 24%
17. 77%
18. 5%
19. 6%
20. 67%
21. d
22. f

23. a
24. g
25. e
26. b
27. c
28. 50, 1/2, 50
29. 10, 1/10, 10
30. 25, 1/4, 25

pages 48–49

1. 63%
2. 30%
3. 55%
4. 25%
5. 50%
6. 20%
7. 60%
8. 33%
9. 6%
10. 35%
11. 74%
12. 36%
13. 62.5%
14. 99.3%
15. 5%
16. 2.5%

Fraction	Decimal	Percent
1/10	0.1	10%
1/2	0.5	50%
3/20	0.15	15%
7/10	0.7	70%
29/100	0.29	29%
71/100	0.71	71%
2/5	0.4	40%
3/5	0.6	60%
9/100	0.09	9%
3/50	0.06	6%
3/8	0.375	37.5%
1/40	0.025	2.5%
1/50	0.02	2%
1 3/10	1.3	130%
723/1000	0.723	72.3%

pages 50–51

1. $\frac{3 \times 10}{10 \times 10} = \frac{30}{100} = 30\%$
2. $\frac{5 \times 10}{10 \times 10} = \frac{50}{100} = 50\%$
3. $\frac{1 \times 25}{4 \times 25} = \frac{25}{100} = 25\%$
4. $\frac{3 \times 25}{4 \times 25} = \frac{75}{100} = 75\%$
5. $\frac{2 \times 25}{4 \times 25} = \frac{50}{100} = 50\%$
6. $\frac{1 \times 20}{5 \times 20} = \frac{20}{100} = 20\%$
7. 50%
8. 60%
9. 25%
10. 12.5%
11. 40%
12. 35%
13. 37.5%
14. 75%
15. 80%

pages 52–53

1. $12.00
2. $25.00
3. $700.00
4. $192.00
5. $630.00
6. $19.50
7. $40,500.00
8. $12.60
9. $100.00
10. $118.90
11. $32
12. 3 pigs
13. $7200 and $7500, $300 greater
14. $5.99
15. $5391; $1797
16. $18,868.50
17. $7547.40

pages 54–55

1. 54 stories
2. 48 heroes
3. 60 percent
4. 224 people
5. 90 people
6. 40%

pages 56–57

1. 40
2. 50
3. 25
4. 40
5. 60
6. 4
7. 5
8. 28
9. 24
10. 36
11. 50
12. 56
13. 75%
14. 75%

Notes

Notes

Notes